Dedication

Tiffanee

My amazing and loving wife. Without her insistence that I go to seminary and her hard work and patience to provide for it, I may have never learned the disciplines or resources to make this study possible. Thank you.

Tim

My dear friend with the most passionate heart to reach the nations that I have ever known. Without his encouragement I would never have thought to publish. Thank you.

> But far be it from me to boast except in the cross of our Lord Jesus Christ, by which the world has been crucified to me, and I to the world. — The Apostle Paul
>
> **Galatians 6:16** [1]

---

[1] All Scripture references in this book are from The Holy Bible, English Standard Version. ESV® Text Edition: 2016. Copyright © 2001 by Crossway Bibles, a publishing ministry of Good News Publishers via www.biblegateway.com

From the Author

Grace vs. "It's Up To Me"

The greatest lie of the enemy and the greatest lie in our hearts is *"it's up to me."*

Dear Reader,

Legalism, grace, self-righteousness, justification, law, freedom. If you have been around the church for any period of time these words are frequently used. However, I have found that so few of us really know what they mean nor do we see their impact on our life and soul.

I grew up in a charismatic church. Legalism, law, etc. was anything that looked like tradition, organs, hymnals, and denominationalism. Grace and freedom were modern worship, spontaneous preaching, and moving in the Spirit. When I was a teenager, I was part of a fundamentalist homeschool curriculum. Grace and freedom was found in being "radical" for Jesus by following a strict standard of holiness — no television, rock music, dating, or wearing denim. When I went to a Baptist seminary, grace was found in expository preaching and it was pointed out to me the charismatics were legalistically unlegalistic. After all, some charismatics said you had to speak in tongues to be saved (a spiritualized rule)!

Thankfully, I had a wise mentor who understood grace. He directed me to study the teachings of Paul and I began to really understand grace vs. legalism. But I still used all the regular terms.

Then something interesting happened. God called me to pastor a church in a county that is 15-20% Amish. Now the Amish are great people with a zeal for a form of godliness. But their whole system of belief is built upon a religious system of rights and wrongs in order to please God and not anger Him. They work very hard to not make a mistake. When they do make a mistake, unbearable shame is ever-present in their consciousness.

It was while living in a community with a sect of Christianity that literally rides around town in their horse-drawn legalism and wear it on their sleeves and bonnets, it suddenly hit me. The core of it all can be summed up in one phrase: legalism says, "it is up to me." Charismatics, fundamentalist, Baptists, Amish, and almost every other belief system that doesn't keep grace and Jesus at its center gradually degrades into a system or way to try to impress God and keep Him happy with us that is "up to me." Now, an anti "it's up to me" message has become the hallmark of my preaching.

Our congregation has heard me say it before, and I will say it again; "the greatest lie of the enemy and the greatest lie in our hearts is 'it's up to me.'" It's up to me to make my destiny, to live the right way, do the right thing, make up for my wrongs, do better, get better, love better. At first it sounds like humility or even responsibility, but in the center of it all is the exact opposite. It is ultimately pride. Deceptive, destructive, pride.

The cornerstone of the message of Jesus is salvation by grace through faith in Him alone. The ultimate expression of faith is that of complete surrender to the work and power of Jesus in our lives. It is the exact opposite of "me." It is Christ alone! It is in surrender that Jesus gets the most glory.

Think about it. Every place where I think something is up to me is a place where I may rob God of glory. If I do it, even if I do it well, I get the glory. If I do it poorly, I get all the blame. But if I surrender to Jesus and the power of His Spirit, I get grace and God gets the glory. How freeing!

Perhaps no book of the Bible explores this concept more concisely than Paul's letter to the church in Galatia. It is here that Paul expresses the power of surrender and grace so eloquently when he says:

"I have been crucified with Christ. It is no longer I who live, but Christ who lives in me. And the life I now live in the flesh I live by faith in the Son of God, who loved me and gave himself for me." — Galatians 2:20

Simply put. It is no longer up to me. I have surrendered. I have died. And the rest of my life I have to give, I do it by faith believing that Jesus will always lead me to the life I am meant to live. It isn't up to me. I live for Jesus!

That is simple grace!

I hope the study of this amazing book will help you come fully into the power of Jesus' grace. May you engage in the freedom of its message and the liberation of your soul! And may you sing the following to its fullest meaning:

Healed and forgiven
Look where my chains are now
Death has no hold on me
Because your grace holds that ground
Once I was broken
But you loved my whole heart through
Sin has no hold on me
Your grace holds me now! [2]

A Few Suggestions for This Study

Allow me to make just a few suggestions on how to get the most out of this study.

First, set aside a ***place and time*** to do the study. You won't need much time — 10-15 minutes a day will be enough on most days. But pick a time. Also, pick a place. Your favorite chair, at the kitchen table with coffee, on your lunch break. This way you will stay committed to it easier.

Second, ***have your Bible***. Most of the entries in this devotional will have you read several verses from your Bible, and then will comment on a selection of verses from that reading. The selections will be included in the devotional, but our goal is for you to study the entire book these next six weeks. So you will need both.

I encourage you to read whatever translation of the Bible you enjoy most. However, in this devotional, we are using the English Standard Version (ESV) unless otherwise mentioned.

Third, I recommend ***something to write with and write on***. A pen or pencil along with a journal will be helpful. There is space to write on many of the entries, but it might not be enough. I have always found that writing just a few short sentences helps me both process with the Holy Spirit and remember what I am learning.

Finally, come with a ***humble and teachable heart***. The essence of simple grace is found in an attitude of humility and surrender. This devotional is not an exhaustive, exposition of every fine theological and grammatical point of the text. So please don't expect it to be. Rather,

---

[2] Whole Heart (Hold Me Now), Joel Houston & Aodhan King, Hillsong United, 2019

be easily impressed and ready to learn from the Holy Spirit. I am writing to provoke your heart to think hard about how grace vs. "It's up to me" really impacts us.

So now, let's begin.

Jeremy M. Gwaltney

Lead Pastor

Harvest Community Church

Goshen, IN

www.hccgoshen.org

Why Did Paul Write Galatians?

"Brothers, you know that some time ago God made a choice among you that the Gentiles might hear from my lips the message of the gospel and believe. God, who knows the heart, showed that he accepted them by giving the Holy Spirit to them, just as he did to us. He did not discriminate between us and them, for he purified their hearts by faith. Now then, why do you try to test God by putting on the necks of Gentiles a yoke that neither we nor our ancestors have been able to bear? No! We believe it is through the grace of our Lord Jesus that we are saved, just as they are."

— *Apostle Peter, Jerusalem Council*

Acts 15:7-11 (NIV)[3]

"It is my judgment, therefore, that we should not make it difficult for the Gentiles who are turning to God.

— *James, The Brother of Jesus, Jerusalem Council*

Acts 15:19 (NIV)

Suggested Bible Reading: Acts 14 - 15

---

[3] All NIV references from Holy Bible, New International Version®, NIV® Copyright ©1973, 1978, 1984. 2011 by Biblica, Inc.® All rights reserved Worldwide. Via www.biblegateway.com

Paul, an apostle—not from men nor through man, but through Jesus Christ and God the Father, who raised him from the dead... To the churches of Galatia: Grace to you and peace ...
— *Galatians 1:1-3*

Before we jump into the study of this amazing book, we need to consider its context. After all, there was a reason that Paul was writing this particular letter to this particular church in the region of Galatia. As you can see from the passage above, he had several key themes...

Paul, an apostle... an apostle — not from men... To the churches of Galatia... Grace to you and peace...

Why did he say those things? What was going on? Where was Galatia anyway? Today, I want you to invest some time in these questions, so you understand the rest of the book better.

The following few pages will help you answer these questions. While it is not exhaustive, or perfect, I hope that it will be helpful to you as you study the incredible message of grace. There are three basic contexts for the book of Galatians. The first is the Historical Context – which deals with things such as who the author was, who the audience was, when it was written, where Galatia was, etc. The second is the Biblical Context – that is how the book fits into the message of the Bible as a whole. Finally, there is the book itself – and that includes things like the attitude of the writer, the content of the book, etc. Below are a few notes on each.

Historical Background

The historical details surrounding the book of Galatians are greatly debated by scholars. Galatia was a portion of the Roman Empire located in what is today modern Turkey. However, it is still debated exactly where in Turkey the book was written.[4]

I believe it is most likely that the Apostle Paul[5] wrote the book of Galatians to the churches of Southern Galatia – probably in the cities of Iconium, Lystra, and Derbe – around AD 48, just prior to the Council of Jerusalem described in Acts 15.[6]

There are two important things to know about this historical context. First, Galatians would probably be Paul's first letter written, demonstrating the depth of Paul's theology from the earliest beginnings of his ministry. Second, if Galatians is written before the Jerusalem Council in Acts 15, it represents tremendous conviction and boldness by Paul. The Council and the content of Galatians deal with very similar topics; the role of circumcision and the Old Testament Law for Christians. While both Acts 15 and Galatians agree in theology, for Paul to write the book before the Council means he was giving theological direction before the entire church agreed upon the decision. This is especially bold considering the fact that Paul says, "any other gospel" should be accursed."

---

[4] Among evangelical scholars, there are traditionally two views about when and to whom the book of Galatians was written. One is that Paul wrote Galatians to the churches of Northern Galatia during the late AD 50s while on his third missionary journey (Acts 18:23-20:38), the second is that he wrote the book to the churches of Southern Galatia around AD 48 prior to the Jerusalem Council of Acts 15 (Acts 14:21-Acts 15:35). It is my opinion that the Southern Galatia view is to be preferred for three primary reasons: 1) nowhere in Acts does it indicate that Paul traveled to Northern Galatia, but Acts does record Paul traveling to the three major cities of Southern Galatia (Iconium, Lystra, and Derbe) on his first missionary journey (Acts 14:1-25). 2) Paul's concern for the Galatians and the debate in the Jerusalem Council of Acts 15 have to do with very similar topics – circumcision and the nature of the Old Testament Law within Christianity. Had Paul written the letter after the Jerusalem Council, it would seem logical that he would have referenced their decision (Acts 15:23-29). 3) Finally, Galatians mentions Paul visiting Jerusalem twice (Gal. 1:18; 2:1) before his second missionary journey, while Acts mentions him visiting Jerusalem three times (Acts 9:26-30; 11:29-30; 15:1-35) before this journey. If Galatians is written before the final visit to Jerusalem (Acts 15), then they agree. If it is written after Acts 15, then it is difficult to account for Paul not mentioning the third trip in Galatians 1-2.

[5] In addition to the mention of Paul's name in verse 1, even liberal scholars agree this book is by Paul – it is perhaps the most agreed upon historical issue in the book.

[6] For more on the Jerusalem Council, continue reading.

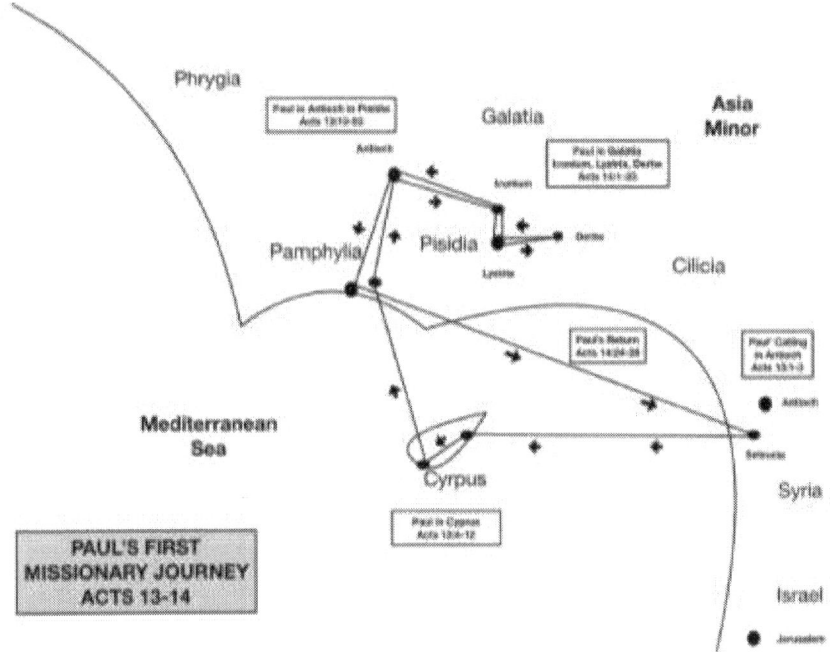

The second key historical aspect of the book of Galatians is the nature of Paul's opponents. There are few books that Paul wrote with such angst and fervor, and very few where Paul attacks his opponents as viciously as in Galatians (Gal. 1:8; 5:12; 6:11-12).

Most likely these opponents are of the same group of teachers mentioned in Acts 15:1-2; who were teaching that "unless you be circumcised, according to the custom taught by Moses, you cannot be saved" (Acts 15:1). Acts 15 reports that Paul and Barnabas, both of whom founded the churches in Galatia, were arguing with these teachers and it was this dispute that lead to the Jerusalem Council. This group of teachers, often called Judaizers, were probably a remnant of the converted Pharisees. In the book of Galatians we can deduce that they were attacking the nature of Paul's apostleship (Gal. 1:1), were attacking the source of his revelation of the gospel (Gal. 1:11-2:10), had greatly infiltrated the Galatian church (Gal. 3:1; 4:11), and were experiencing less persecution than those of pure Christianity (Gal. 6:12).

What seems to have happened in the background of this book is that Paul and Barnabas returned from their missionary journey where they founded the churches in southern Galatia and had begun to see Jews and Gentiles come to Christ (Acts 14:8-28). Upon returning to Antioch, they began to debate the sect of the Judaizers over the exact nature of salvation (Acts 15:1-5). Paul then learned that this sect had followed him to Galatia, and were beginning to lead the churches astray. So he wrote the letter of Galatians to those churches to warn them of the "false gospel" of the Judaizers. In the meantime, the apostles and elders of the Jerusalem church decided it was time to end the debate once and for all and summoned Paul and Barnabas, along with the Judaizers, to appear in Jerusalem to debate the issue (Acts 15:8-35).

Biblical Background

The major issue regarding Biblical context that is key for understanding the book of Galatians is the issue of circumcision and Paul's understanding of the Old Testament.

Circumcision for the Jews was a symbol of their covenant with Yahweh and the mark of being the chosen people of God. It is first seen in Genesis 17, when God instructs Abraham to be circumcised and to circumcise all of his offspring as a "sign" of the covenant between Abraham and Yahweh. This covenant was that the "seed" of Abraham would bring "blessings" to all nations (Gen. 12), and become a "great nation." Circumcision was later instituted by Moses in Exodus 12 and written into the Law of Moses in Leviticus 12. For the Jewish people, to be a "son of Abraham" was to be saved, and this was interpreted in Paul's day to include circumcision. By the time of the New Testament, it seems clear that circumcision had become more than a "sign" of the covenant, and was almost a "means" of salvation. This was the basic teaching of the Judaizers – Christ and circumcision (keeping the Law of Moses) brings salvation.

Paul's argument in Galatians is essentially one of originality – what is first, is original; and what is original takes precedent over all. Paul rightly notes that Abraham was "saved" when he "believed God"[7] in Genesis 15:6, and that the promise of a great nation was given to a singular seed – not just the entire nation (Genesis 12). For Paul, Abraham's faith takes precedent over all other customs because it came

---

[7] The word "believe" in Hebrew is essentially the same word used by the New Testament writers for "faith."

before circumcision or the giving of the Law. Thus, Paul sees the gospel of salvation by faith alone in Christ (the promised Seed of Abraham) as a continuation of the original covenant of Abraham. Circumcision is secondary, and has no saving power. Indeed, it is interesting that at the end of the Torah (The five books or "Law" of Moses; Genesis, Exodus, Leviticus, Numbers, and Deuteronomy), Moses says the following:

> *"And now, Israel, what does the LORD your God require of you, but to fear the LORD your God, to walk in all his ways, to love him, to serve the LORD your God with all your heart and with all your soul, and to keep the commandments and statutes of the LORD... **Circumcise** therefore the foreskin of **your heart**, and be no longer stubborn."*
> *– Deuteronomy 10:12-13,16*

And later ...

> *"And the LORD your God will **circumcise your heart** and the heart of your offspring, so that you will love the LORD your God with all your heart and with all your soul, that you may live."*
> *– Deuteronomy 30:6*

It is important to note that in both of these passages God is primarily after an inner work of the heart – not an outward symbol. It is faith in God and the fear of the Lord that changes a man's heart, not his actions. This is essentially Paul's argument, unless you have faith and your heart is changed by the life, death, and resurrection of Jesus Christ – the promised Seed – you cannot be a son of Abraham and there is no salvation. All outward actions not done in faith are ultimately worthless for salvation.

The sole issue of faith and the work of Christ is Paul's major point. While the Law of Moses is good and needed (Gal. 3:15-4:7), to say that the Law or circumcision saves is dangerous. For Paul, the degree to which something has to be added to the work of Christ, is the degree to which Christ's death and resurrection are insufficient to save us. Thus, to participate in those works as a means of salvation is to insult the work of Christ on the cross. That is why Paul says it is "no gospel," because to say that our works save us in anyway is to "nullify the grace of God" (Gal. 2:21).

Galatians – About the Letter

Finally, the content of the book itself. There are several things that we should note while reading this book.

First, note the tone of the book. Paul is vehement, passionate, and, quite honestly, very upset. Watching the church he help to found turn from the true gospel renders him a feeling of "working in vain." Paul's emotion is evident from the start of the letter. Typical letters in the New Testament begin with an address (Gal. 1:1-2); they are then followed by a blessing (Gal. 1:3-5) and then are followed by a thanksgiving section.[8] But Paul skips this and goes right to "I am amazed that you are so quickly deserting Him…" (Gal. 1:6). This would have sent shockwaves into the ears of the Galatian readers and emphasized the importance of the letter's content to their salvation in Christ.

Second, the book almost exactly breaks down with four chapters of theological underpinning and two chapters of practical application. This is typical of Paul's writings – in his mind, good theology is lived out practically. Thus, our life exhibits our theology. That is why he takes so much time to lay the foundation of his argument so that we can indeed practically live in the "freedom of Christ."

With all of this in mind, let's jump into our study.[9]

---

[8] See Philippians 1:1-5, Colossians 1:1-4, 1 Thessalonians 1:1-5, 2 Thessalonians 1:1-4; all include an address, blessing and thanksgiving in their opening clauses.

[9] The information used for this background essay was taken from the following resources:
An Introduction to the New Testament, 2nd Edition, by D.A. Carson and Douglass Moo, Zondervan, 1992, 2005
The Expositors Bible Commentary on Galatians, Volume 10. edited by Frank E. Gaebelein, Zondervan, 1976
The New International Greek New Testament Commentary on Galatians, F.F. Bruce, Eerdmans Press, 1982
New Testament Commentary*,* William Hendriksen, Baker Books, 1968
Lectures by Dr. Scott Kellum, associate professor of New Testament and Greek at Southeastern Baptist Theological Seminary in Wake Forrest, NC

Week 1

Galatians 1:1-2:14

Simple Grace

Jesus Doing for Me What I Can't Do on My Own

Grace to you and peace from God our Father and the Lord Jesus Christ, who gave himself for our sins to deliver us from the present evil age, according to the will of our God and Father, to whom be the glory forever and ever. Amen.
— Galatians 1:3-5

Week 1, Day 1

Grace to you and peace from God our Father and the Lord Jesus Christ, who gave himself for our sins to deliver us from the present evil age, according to the will of our God and Father, to whom be the glory forever and ever. Amen.

— **Galatians 1:3-5**

Bible Reading: Galatians 1:1-5

Take just a moment to ponder the words above.

Grace to you and peace from God our Father and the Lord Jesus Christ,

Grace and peace are the subjects of Paul's writing. They are the deepest realities that our soul needs. Yet, don't miss where it is coming from — God the Father and our Lord, Jesus Christ. How did we obtain this grace?

who gave himself for our sins

By Jesus giving Himself for us. His death dealt with all our sins. All the death in our lives. All our hurts, insufficiencies, mistakes, heartaches. He gave himself for them all. How did this sacrifice work?

to deliver us from the present evil age,

He delivers us from this present evil age. Have you noticed that this age is evil and wants to trap us in its evil? Jesus' sacrifice and grace bring the freedom from the age by allowing us to access the Kingdom of God that will come in the next age. By grace, we get to taste the freedom of heaven now. Why did this happen?

according to the will of our God and Father,

Because God wanted it to happen. Get this, God didn't want heaven without you. So He made a way for you to taste heaven both now and forever. What is the fundamental reality of heaven? An unhindered relationship with Jesus. How can we be sure of this reality?

to whom be the glory forever and ever. Amen.

Because God's fame is at stake! He secured us so He can get the glory. Thus, we are instruments of that glory! The more we jump into the grace of Jesus the more glory God gets and the more freedom we feel from this present evil age. WOW!

Bible Reading Question:

Is there anything from the reading that speaks to you today? If so, what is it?

Points for Pondering and Prayer:

Spend some time thanking God for His grace.

What is one area of your life where you would like to experience more freedom?

Week 1, Day 2

Bible Reading: Galatians 1:6-10

I am astonished that you are so quickly deserting him who called you in the grace of Christ and are turning to a different gospel ...

— **Galatians 1:6**

These words would have been shocking to the Galatians. Shocking for several reasons. At this point in a classic Roman letter, there should have been a thanksgiving, but Paul just launches into his concern.

Second, he doesn't give them the benefit of the doubt. The Galatians' problem wasn't an accident, it was abandonment. All the beauty of grace found in verses 4 and 5 is now being "deserted."

Notice, though, who Paul says is being deserted — Jesus, "him who called you in grace."

Jesus is the central and all-consuming focus of grace. It is not the behavior, or belief system, or the morality that the Galatians were abandoning by their actions. They were abandoning Jesus. Grace is always about the relationship, the love, and the surrender to Jesus.

And Paul knows that without a whole-hearted loyalty to Jesus the Galatians are sunk!

So, what about you? Are you clinging to the person of grace? Or relying on yourself?

Bible Reading Question:

Is there anything from the reading that speaks to you today? If so, what is it?

Points for Pondering and Prayer:

Take just a moment and ask the Holy Spirit to reveal anything in you that is taking the place of Jesus. If something comes up, give it over to Jesus.

Ask Jesus if there is anything you need to surrender to Him.

Week 1, Day 3

<u>Bible Reading</u>: Galatians 1:11-24

What was going on here? As I mentioned in Day 1, Paul was coming under attack by a group of converted Pharisees who were saying that you had to love Jesus and completely obey the Old Testament Law in order to be saved. They were threatened by Paul's preaching that the message of Jesus was a message of grace by faith alone. So in addition to teaching something different, they attacked Paul's credibility by saying that Paul was given his message by men, not by the Holy Spirit. They also probably distorted the nature of Paul's relationship with the leaders of the first church in Jerusalem — James (Jesus' brother) and Cephas (Peter). So, Paul began his letter by setting the record straight on his relationship with the leaders of the church, his conversion, and his conviction of the message of grace that Jesus taught.

His key point — "I was the greatest Pharisee of them all. I met Jesus. None of the things I did as a Pharisee mattered. Jesus' grace was all that mattered." This grace was enough for the best of the Jews and the worst of Gentiles. He then went into his transformation from killing the followers of Jesus, to proclaiming the love of Jesus. How did the followers of Jesus respond to his transformation?

And they glorified God because of me.

— Galatians 1:24

That is the power of grace. Jesus' love and grace can take God's enemy and make him the most influential ambassador for His message of all time. If God can do it for Paul, He can do it in you.

So, what about you? Is there a place in your life you think is too hopeless for God? Do you believe that He can make you a trophy of His glory?

Bible Reading Question:

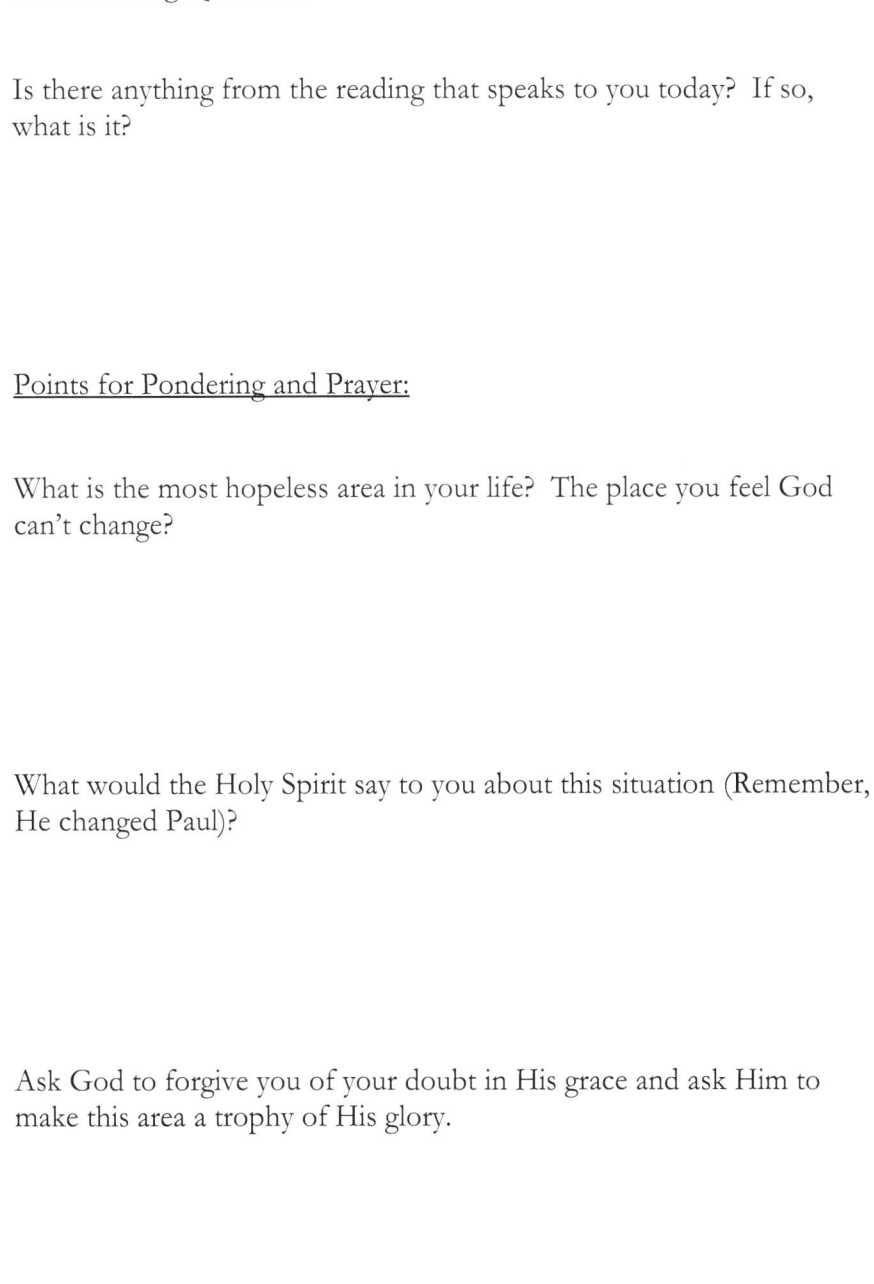

Is there anything from the reading that speaks to you today? If so, what is it?

Points for Pondering and Prayer:

What is the most hopeless area in your life? The place you feel God can't change?

What would the Holy Spirit say to you about this situation (Remember, He changed Paul)?

Ask God to forgive you of your doubt in His grace and ask Him to make this area a trophy of His glory.

Week 1, Day 4

<u>Bible Reading:</u> Galatians 2:1-14

Yet because of false brothers secretly brought in—who slipped in to spy out our freedom that we have in Christ Jesus, so that they might bring us into slavery— to them we did not yield in submission even for a moment, so that the truth of the gospel might be preserved for you.

— Galatians 2:4-5

Oh, the power of the "it's up to me" lie. It is really hard to exchange it for the freedom of simple grace.

In our passage today, Paul continues to argue for the legitimacy of his message of grace in Jesus. He described how he came to begin ministering, how he discussed his theology with the leaders of the church in Jerusalem, how they welcomed Titus, one of Paul's disciples and probably the namesake for one of Paul's letters in the New

Testament, without requiring him to be circumcised according to the Old Testament Law, and how they all "gave the right hand of fellowship to… me."

And yet, the Jewish tradition of acceptance by obedience to a Law was so strong, even Peter fell into its trap when he came to visit the Jewish-Gentile church in Antioch. Paul had to rebuke him for acting outside of the faith by only eating with Jews. It was an attack on the freedom of grace!

Ultimately, that is what the "it's up to me" lie is — an attack on our freedom to enjoy Jesus. Instead of running into the arms of a loving Savior who has forgiven us and empowered us to enjoy our lives to the fullest, this lie turns God into a contract negotiator. "You will be accepted if you agree to abide by the contract in this way. If you break the contract, then you are responsible for all the problems in life."

True freedom comes by enjoying Jesus and responding to His love!

You are accepted, you are loved — now love back fiercely.

This is why Paul said so strongly, "to them we did not yield submission even for a moment." Let's be like Paul!

Bible Reading Question:

Is there anything from the reading that speaks to you today? If so, what is it?

Points for Pondering and Prayer:

Are there areas in your life where you feel like you have to impress God or that you are afraid you will let God down? What are they?

Confess those things to God and refuse to submit to their slavery.

Ask God to fill you with His Holy Spirit and teach you new levels of freedom in His grace.

Week 1, Day 5

<u>Bible Reading</u>: Galatians 2:7-10

*Only, they asked us to remember the poor,
the very thing I was eager to do.*
— Galatians 2:10

Social justice. Starting in the early 2000s, this became a huge issue among churches in America. In fact, it divides many churches to this day. Churches that identify as "progressive" often point to the command to care for the poor and outcast and say that Jesus' Gospel must help these groups or it is worthless. Those churches identifying as "evangelical" or "conservative" tend to say that the Gospel is about "heart change." After all, they may ask, what good is giving a poor person bread if they face an eternity in hell?

So which is it?

Well, like so many other issues when it comes to following Jesus, it is a bit of both. Here we see it in live action. Paul is telling Peter and James and others of his amazing revelation of the grace of Jesus. A grace that goes beyond an "it's up to me" list of rules to gain God's approval, and a grace that even allows the Gentiles to come to know Him. Jesus dies to change our hearts, save our souls, and make us spiritually alive! We are changed because of Jesus. Then Paul essentially says, "what do you think?"

"They asked us to remember the poor." That was their response. Wow. Think about the implications here.

Yes, the simple grace of Jesus saves us from sin, changes our hearts, makes us alive to the things of God. It is primarily a spiritual exchange. Jesus died to save our souls and change our hearts from a sinful state to a righteous state.

But what is the evidence of a true heart change? It is found in loving those who don't have the heart nor means to love us back. "Remember the poor." Who are the poor? Those who can never really offer us anything. When we give we receive nothing in return. Paul, the leaders of the church, and the newly converted Gentiles who are able to give, all stand in the place of power providing for the needs of those who stand in the place of weakness. The poor have nothing to offer.

"Remember the poor" is a physical example of the spiritual reality of the work of Jesus. After all, Jesus was spiritually rich and gave to us the spiritually poor. And we had nothing of value to offer Him in return. And yet He gave His life for us anyway. Jesus' sacrifice to save our souls made spiritual bankrupt people whole again. When our hearts are changed by this gift of salvation, we have the opportunity to show the world a real example of this love when we provide for those who can't give us anything in return. That is why the early church believed so strongly that we should "remember the poor." It is a simple expression of simple grace.

Bible Reading Question:

Is there anything from the reading that speaks to you today? If so, what is it?

Points for Pondering and Prayer:

Do you see yourself as spiritually bankrupt with God as your provider? Ask the Holy Spirit to reveal this to you.

Are you generous with the poor? Do you give time and financial resources to care for those in need in your community? If not, how can you begin?

Week 2

Galatians 2:15-3:14

The Life of Grace

Life Empowered by the Holy Spirit

Let me ask you only this: Did you receive the Spirit by works of the law or by hearing with faith? Are you so foolish? Having begun by the Spirit, are you now being perfected by the flesh?
— Galatians 3:2-3

Week 2, Day 1

We ourselves are Jews by birth and not Gentile sinners; yet we know that a person is not justified by works of the law but through faith in Jesus Christ, so we also have believed in Christ Jesus, in order to be justified by faith in Christ and not by works of the law, because by works of the law no one will be justified.

— **Galatians 2:15-16**

Having spent the last chapter and a half defending himself, Paul turns the next few chapters into an explanation of Jesus' message of simple grace. This is his thesis statement: through chapter four he will talk about how we are "justified," the inability of the Law to save us, and the difference between Jews and Gentiles (all non-Jews) in the plan of God.

Notice what he says first, the Jews know that they can't be justified by the Law. In other words, Jews know that they can't be "made right" in the eyes of God by following all the rules and traditions of the Old Testament. They know there must be more.

It is significant to note that in the Acts 15 discussion of grace vs. the Law, Peter says this about the Old Testament Law:

And God, who knows the heart, bore witness to them, by giving [the Gentiles] the Holy Spirit just as he did to us, and he made no distinction between us and them, having cleansed their hearts by faith. Now, therefore, why are you putting God to the test by placing a yoke on the neck of the disciples that neither our fathers nor we have been able to bear? But we believe that we will be saved through the grace of the Lord Jesus, just as they will."

— **Acts 15:8-11**

The Law, the rules, the traditions, the "right way," the "it's up to me to obey," are a burden that the Jews "have [not] been able to bear." What is the only hope for salvation? The "giving of the Holy Spirit" that empowers the "grace of the Lord Jesus."

There it is. It isn't up to me or something I can do. Grace that makes me acceptable to God in ALL THINGS comes by Jesus' gift of the Holy Spirit and His grace. When I surrender to Him by faith, I am made right and acceptable — *nothing else is needed.*

Points for Pondering and Prayer:

Do you consider the Holy Spirit to be part of your everyday life? If not, you are an easy target for the "it's up to me" trap.

Ask God to fill you with His Holy Spirit today and begin teaching you what it means to rely upon Him by faith.

Ask the Holy Spirit to show you the burdens you have because you have not relied upon the grace of Jesus.

Week 2, Day 2

<u>Bible Reading</u>: Galatians 2:17-21

> *For if I rebuild what I tore down, I prove myself to be a transgressor... And the life I now live in the flesh I live by faith in the Son of God, who loved me and gave himself for me. I do not nullify the grace of God, for if righteousness were through the law, then Christ died for no purpose.*
> **— Galatians 2:18, 20b-21**

Paul here explains exactly why trusting in our own ability to impress God is so devastating and how hard it is to overcome. If it is truly up to us — in any way — to make ourselves right before God, we have a problem.

"If I rebuild what I tore down, I prove myself a transgressor." Paul is basically saying that if we experience grace and freedom from the Law — coming to God by grace — but then later continue to try to come to God on our own, we prove that we are in need of grace. The pull of "I have to do it myself, I have to make my life right" is so strong that even after tasting the grace of God, we fall into the trap.

But here is the hopelessness of that trap. "If righteousness were through the law, then Christ died for no purpose." Think about the nature of sacrificing someone's life for a greater cause. In a military exercise in which casualties will occur, we feel that those deaths had purpose if the operation secured a greater opportunity for victory and freedom. However, if we send troops into battle, and there was a way to secure victory without loss of life, we are OUTRAGED at those meaningless deaths.

Paul is saying the same thing here. If there were ANY OTHER WAY to secure our salvation and freedom from sin other than the death of Jesus, then Jesus would have died in vain. Instead of a noble sacrifice ordered by a loving Father, Jesus' actions would be a wasted life ordered by a heartless butcher.

Yet, when we try to impress God by our actions, obey Him to get His attention, or rely on our actions to earn our place in His family, we are essentially doing the same thing — telling Jesus His sacrifice wasn't needed, we got this on our own, "it's up to me" and I will do it my way. What a shame. What bondage.

The only solution for sin, bondage, and forgiveness is living "by faith in the Son of God." Faith is the ultimate expression of surrender. I can't do life the right way, I HAVE TO HAVE Jesus.

Bible Reading Question:

Is there anything from the reading that speaks to you today? If so, what is it?

Points for Pondering and Prayer:

Ask the Holy Spirit if there are any places in your life where you have not surrendered to the grace of God? Think big and small: job performance, parenting skills, identity, freedom from shame. What are you holding onto and what have you surrendered by faith?

Pray and, perhaps, journal about it. What is the Holy Spirit asking you to do?

Week 2, Day 3

Bible Reading: Galatians 3:1-6

Let me ask you only this: Did you receive the Spirit by works of the law or by hearing with faith? Are you so foolish? Having begun by the Spirit, are you now being perfected by the flesh?

— Galatians 3:2-3

This may be the most significant verse of Galatians for me personally. It speaks directly to the relationship between grace and my own self-effort.

Paul is basically saying this; do you remember your salvation experience? Did receiving the love and grace of Jesus come as a spiritual experience (powered by the Holy Spirit)? Or did it come because you finally did the right things? Well... if you entered God's family by spiritual faith, why would living in God's family be anything different?

For me, this was so hard to learn. I believed I was saved by putting faith in what Jesus did for me. But then I thought I had to do all the "right things" to be a "good Christian" in my regular life. I lived like I was forgiven by faith but accepted by my obedience and effort. Paul calls this "foolish." It is ALL supposed to be grace by faith.

Think about how you came to know Jesus. Most likely you realized that you felt hopeless or that your weaknesses, sin, and shortcomings were too great for you. You cried out to Jesus and surrendered your life to Him by faith. You knew that you were a new person because you could feel in your spirit that His Holy Spirit was changing your life and accepting you.

sin + repentance + faith + forgiveness = simple [saving] grace.

Just like it worked that way in the BIG moment of your salvation, it is supposed to work that way in the thousands of little moments in which we need little saving every day. Feel lost in what to do at work? Tell Jesus you can't do it, ask for wisdom, surrender your decisions to Him, experience grace. Feel overwhelmed as a mom? Tell Jesus, ask for help, surrender to Him, experience grace. Made a mistake, backsliding? Repent, call out to Jesus, experience grace and forgiveness. Facing overwhelming bondage? Call out to Jesus, surrender by faith, experience the grace to say "no." This is the life of grace, empowered by the Holy Spirit we are called to live each and every moment of our lives. A simple grace empowered by Him.

Bible Reading Question:

Is there anything from the reading that speaks to you today? If so, what is it?

Points for Pondering and Prayer:

Where do you need God's grace today?

Pray, surrender, put your faith in Jesus, receive grace.

Week 2, Day 4

<u>Bible Reading:</u> Galatians 3:6-9

And the Scripture, foreseeing that God would justify the Gentiles by faith, preached the gospel beforehand to Abraham, saying, "In you shall all the nations be blessed."

— Galatians 3:8

Paul now shifts to the second part of his argument — that salvation by grace through faith was ALWAYS God's plan. Case in point — Abraham's salvation.

You see the Jews were saying that to be part of the faith in Jesus, you had to keep the Law and be circumcised because Abraham was circumcised. To be saved was to be "Jewish" and to be "Jewish" was to be the "son of Abraham," because all of the Jews were descendants of Abraham and given a covenant command to keep the Law of Moses. Therefore, you could not be a part of the covenant with the sons of Abraham unless you believed in Jesus, were circumcised and kept the Law. Therefore, all non-Jews, or Gentiles, had to submit to these requirements. It was the Jewish way.

But Paul is going to smash the belief system. His argument? Abraham was justified by faith BEFORE the Law and before his circumcision. Why? Because God wanted to save all people everywhere.

A simple timeline bears this out. God calls Abraham in Genesis 12. Why? To be a blessing to all nations (Gen. 12:3, Gal. 3:8). God then promises an "heir" to Abraham who will establish a nation as numerous as the stars in the sky in Genesis 15. Abraham "believed God" (faith) and God "counted it to him as righteousness" (salvation) in Genesis 15:6 (Gal. 3:6). When was Abraham circumcised, the covenant that symbolized obedience to the Law? Not until Genesis 17, more than 14 years after he received God's righteousness by faith. Oh yeah, Abraham never received the Law of Moses. That came more than 400 years after Abraham's righteousness by faith.

Paul's point? Abraham was saved by faith. Not by circumcision. Not by the Old Testament Law. Why was he saved by faith? So that people of all nations could enter into the blessing God promised him — not just his biological descendants. Simple grace — faith in the work of God to save us — has always been God's plan and it was God's plan for all people. There is no reason to go back to dutiful obedience of the passing covenant that was the Old Testament Law. We are part of God's family by FAITH.

Bible Reading Question:

Is there anything from the reading that speaks to you today? If so, what is it?

Points for Pondering and Prayer:

Since God's plan has always been to save the nations, spend some time praying for missionaries you know overseas.

Spend time praying for the more than two billion people on Earth who still have no knowledge of Simple Grace.

Week 2, Day 5

<u>Bible Reading</u>: Galatians 3:10-14

For all who rely on works of the law are under a curse... Christ redeemed us from the curse of the law by becoming a curse for us...

— Galatians 3:10a, 12a

Everyone who submits to the "It's up to me" lie is living in the bondage of a curse. I like how the Message Translation interprets this verse 10, "And that means that anyone who tries to live by his own effort, independent of God, is doomed to failure."

God is perfect and God is eternal. Because of the curse of sin, the only way to "earn" our way into His acceptance it to live eternally perfect. We are doomed! No one is perfect.

This means that when we try on our own to please God, when we do it ourselves, when we live like pleasing God is up to me — we invite the curse of being eternally perfect on our lives. We take on the pressure of having to measure up to God. What a disaster! What a failing wish! What a curse!

How do we find freedom? It is given to us by Jesus. He is eternal, and He lived perfectly. Fully satisfying all that is necessary to be acceptable to God. He was God's Son after all; in whom God was "well pleased."

Then, being eternally perfect, He submitted Himself to a curse. Dying on a tree. Dying while innocent. Taking the curse of death, the curse of the Law, the punishment and judgment of our sin. Having submitted to this curse, and then defeating it by rising from the dead, He offers that victory to us by faith.

The life of faith is the opposite of living under the curse of our actions. It is submitting all things to the glory of Jesus by trusting Him fully in every aspect of our lives. His glory becomes our glory and His perfection becomes our redemption.

Bible Reading Question:

Is there anything from the reading that speaks to you today? If so, what is it?

Points for Pondering and Prayer:

What are the failures in your life that you are most ashamed of?

Have you tried to make up or compensate for those failures on your own? Does it feel like a curse?

Take some time today talking to the Holy Spirit about your failures and how you feel about them. Confess and surrender them to Him and ask Him to fill you with grace and acceptance.

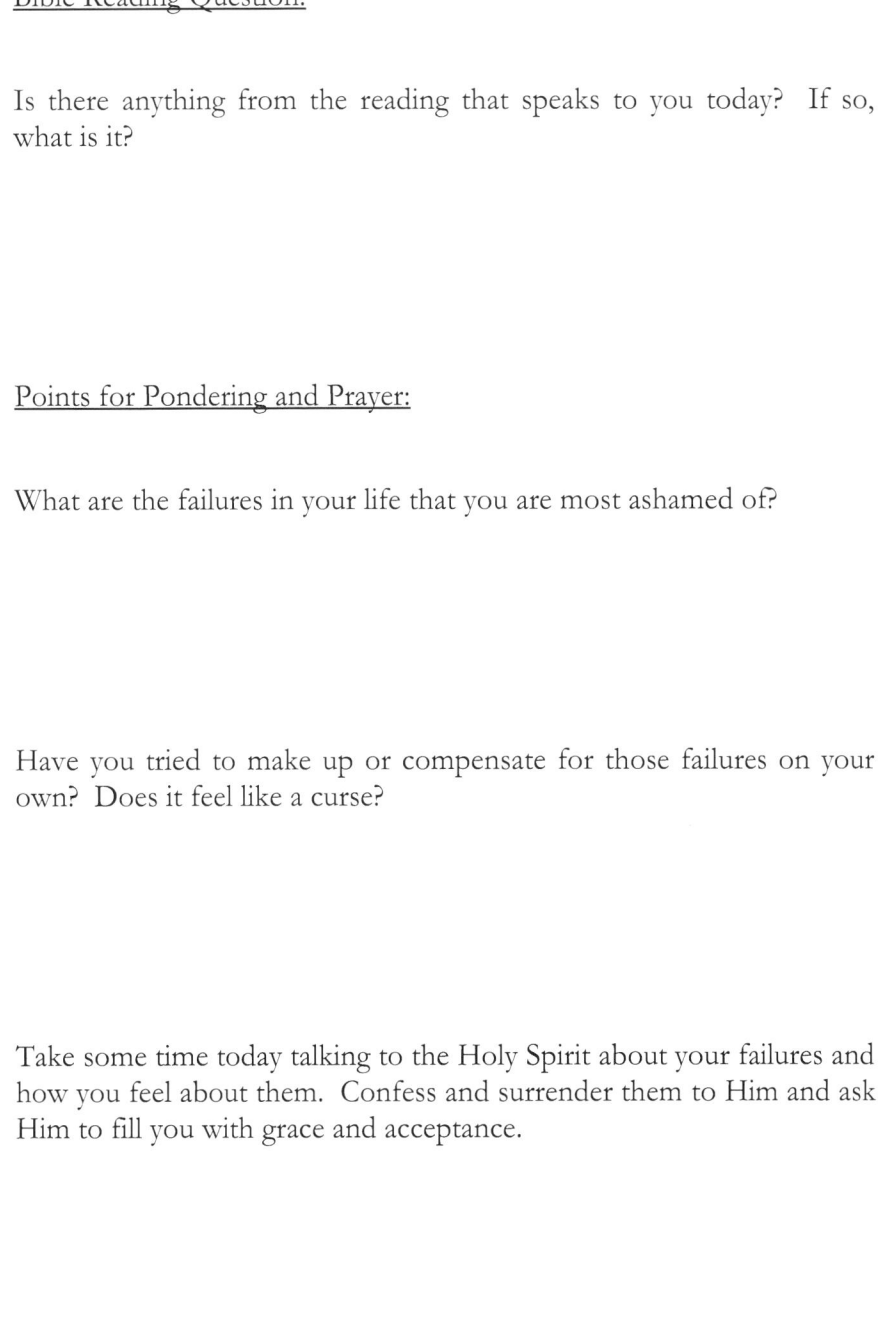

Week 3

Galatians 3:15-4:7

The Plan of Grace

Grace for All People was God's Plan All Along

... for in Christ Jesus you are all sons of God, through faith...And if you are Christ's, then you are Abraham's offspring, heirs according to promise.
— Galatians 2:26, 29

Week 3, Day 1

Bible Reading: Galatians 3:15-17

This is what I mean: the law, which came 430 years afterward, does not annul a covenant previously ratified by God, so as to make the promise void.

— Galatians 3:17

Paul continues to emphasize that God's plan all along was to offer salvation to all of the world through faith in the work of His Son. This paragraph of Scripture is one of the most important paragraphs in understanding the message of purpose in our Old Testament. Here is how Paul breaks it down:

- God came to Abraham and made a promise, a covenant, that through his "offspring" God was going to save the whole world by granting righteousness through faith.

- The word "offspring" in Genesis 12 was not plural, but singular. This was a promise of Jesus. And through belief in this promise, Abraham was counted righteous.

- More than 400 years later, God gave Abraham's descendants the Law to show them how to live as His people — a promise to the Jews. But the Law was not a promise of righteousness.

- The Law was given later and is therefore insufficient to save you. Thus, it is NOT greater than the promise given to Abraham to save us through Jesus.

Grace is superior to effort. Superior in its requirement (full surrender), in its promise (it came first), in its fulfillment (Jesus vs. a people), and in its scope (the whole earth vs. one nation). It was always God's plan! What a powerful thought. If you are living in the grace of God, you were ALWAYS part of His plan!

Bible Reading Question:

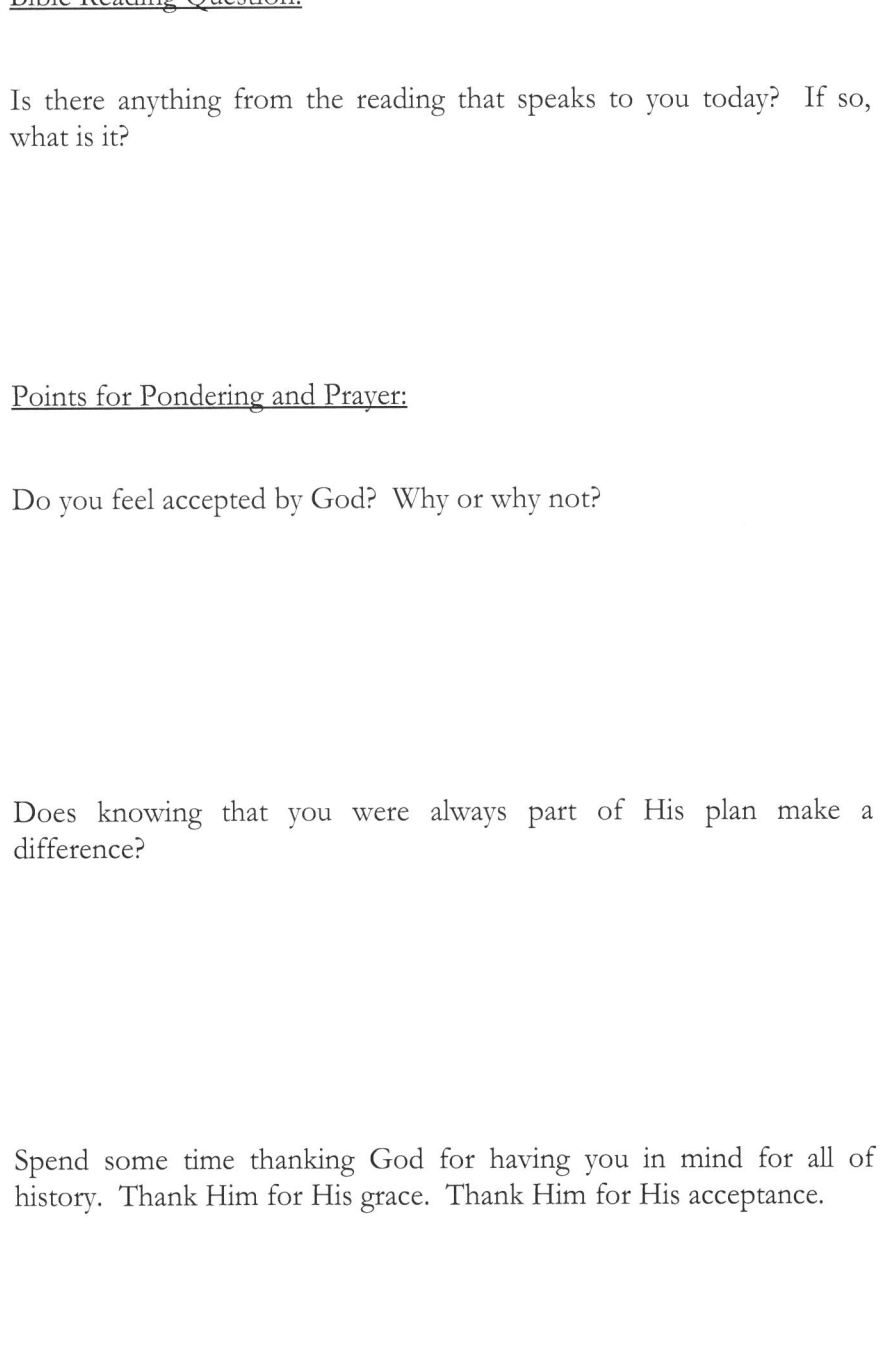

Is there anything from the reading that speaks to you today? If so, what is it?

Points for Pondering and Prayer:

Do you feel accepted by God? Why or why not?

Does knowing that you were always part of His plan make a difference?

Spend some time thanking God for having you in mind for all of history. Thank Him for His grace. Thank Him for His acceptance.

Week 3, Day 2

Why then the law? It was added because of transgressions, until the offspring should come to whom the promise had been made, and it was put in place through angels by an intermediary. Now an intermediary implies more than one, but God is one.

— **Galatians 3:19-20**

Paul continues his discussion by answering the question, "If God's plan was to save everyone by faith, why did He have the law?" Paul is eventually going to say that the right time for humanity hadn't come yet (Gal. 4:4). But until that time, the Law was given to the descendants of Abraham (the Jews) for an important reason — because of transgression.

In other words, for the thousands of years before the Law, God had related to some on the basis of relationship and faith. Adam, Seth, Enoch, Noah, Melchizedek, Abraham, Jacob, Joseph, etc. had all known God and "believed" (had faith) in Him. While it was not a perfect relationship (the fullness of the Holy Spirit had not come), it was still a relationship of faith. They never kept all the parts of the Law, but they did lean into God to learn how to live for Him.

However, when the Jews came out of Egypt, things changed. They were not given to faith and belief the way their forefathers had been. As such, they were constantly missing the heart of God in their lifestyles and were not responding in faith. Since God had chosen them to represent Him to the world until the coming of Jesus, He did something about this transgression. He gave them the Law to show them what "living for God" needed to look like in the ancient world.

But get this. The Law was erected where a life of faith should have been. It was added because of disobedience. Adam, Seth, Enoch, Noah, Melchizedek, Abraham, Jacob, Joseph, etc. had not needed this Law to live for God. They had not always obeyed, but they had always found faith. The result of this new agreement was that it was doomed from the beginning. The Law could never rescue anyone from the sin in their hearts because it was given to simply show us the sin in our hearts.

The Law would last "until the offspring should come" — until Jesus. He is the only one who can change our hearts by the Holy Spirit allowing us to walk in a pleasing relationship with God by faith. That is simple grace.

Points for Pondering and Prayer:

What laws do you live by? Places where you have said, "I will never do that" or "I will always do this" or "I won't ever be like that person?"

Why have you made these statements? Is it because you are trying to be better, or is it a pathway to grace?

Spend some time asking the Holy Spirit to reveal the "secret laws" you have written to make yourself more pleasing to God. Ask Him to reveal what is there because of grace and what is there because of law. Then ask for His grace to cover you.

Week 3, Day 3

Is the law then contrary to the promises of God? Certainly not! For if a law had been given that could give life, then righteousness would indeed be by the law. But the Scripture imprisoned everything under sin, so that the promise by faith in Jesus Christ might be given to those who believe.

— Galatians 3:21-22

Paul continues with his argument by asking if the Law is against God's promise to Abraham. He says, "no." Rather, it actually enhances the power of the promise!

The simple reality is that people have been doomed since the Fall in the Garden of Eden (Genesis 3). After all, it just took one generation before family was killing their own family (Genesis 4). The bondage of our sin was felt in the reign of death on the earth (Genesis 5). Even though there were people who met with and had a relationship with God, most of humanity was living under the reality of death because of their actions against God.

The Law held up a mirror so that mankind could see their sin more clearly. That is why Paul says, "Scripture imprisoned everything under sin." It gave a name to the bondage mankind was already under — the prison of sin. Here is the key point — the Law imprisons. The Law does not give freedom.

Why is that important? Because it demonstrates the power of Jesus' freedom all the more. Jesus is the one who delivers us from the bondage of our sin. And that happens by believing Him. The Law becomes the backdrop of bondage in which Jesus' freedom shines so brightly. We see our sin, we see our hopelessness, then we see our hope — Jesus.

Points for Pondering and Prayer:

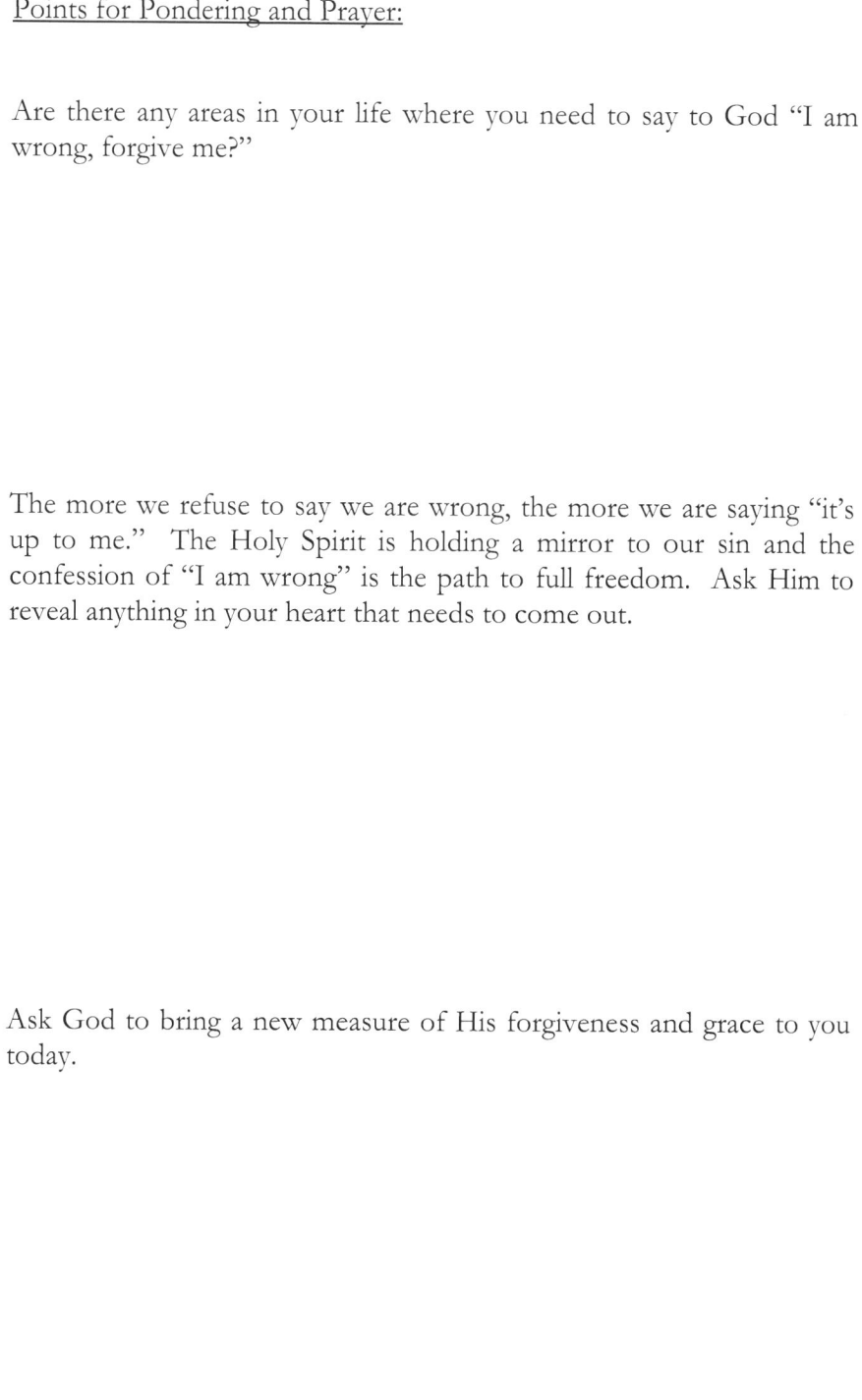

Are there any areas in your life where you need to say to God "I am wrong, forgive me?"

The more we refuse to say we are wrong, the more we are saying "it's up to me." The Holy Spirit is holding a mirror to our sin and the confession of "I am wrong" is the path to full freedom. Ask Him to reveal anything in your heart that needs to come out.

Ask God to bring a new measure of His forgiveness and grace to you today.

Week 3, Day 4

Bible Reading: Galatians 3:23-29

... for in Christ Jesus you are all sons of God, through faith...And if you are Christ's, then you are Abraham's offspring, heirs according to promise.

— Galatians 2:26, 29

One of the most sinister traps of the "it's up to me" lie of the Law is that it creates a grading system. If I do this, God likes me. If I pray this much, give this much, avoid this sin, etc. It also creates classifications of holiness. Have you ever heard the phrase, "he's preaching to the choir?" The implication is that the choir are the "holy people" who do not need to hear the message because they already know. It's a ranking system.

Preacher, missionary, prophet, intercessor; Mennonite, Baptist, Presbyterian, Charismatic; Republican, Democrat, Independent — we all have a measurement for our rank with God. In Paul's day, it was "Jew, a son of Abraham." This was the chosen race, the keepers of the Law, the favorites of God (at least in their minds).

But the cross levels all of humanity.

At the foot of the cross there is only one type of person — a sinner. Your actions, your rank, your intentions, your family, your tradition mean nothing at the foot of the cross. Only your need for Jesus.

When we surrender by faith to Jesus, we become sons of God — part of His family. Not based on our actions or rank, but based on surrender and faith. This is grace and this was the original blessing to Abraham. That was the promise to the world.

Paul is telling us here that the true "sons of Abraham" are those who come into the promise of faith in Jesus. That is the only status that matters. The status given us by simple grace.

Bible Reading Question:

Is there anything from the reading that speaks to you today? If so, what is it?

Points for Pondering and Prayer:

Are there areas in your life where you take pride or your identity from? What are they?

Do they compete with God's identity over you?

Ask the Holy Spirit to truly reveal to you your status as a child of God. Enjoy the simple grace.

Week 3, Day 5

Bible Reading: Galatians 4:1-7

And because you are sons, God has sent the Spirit of his Son into our hearts, crying, "Abba! Father!" So, you are no longer a slave, but a son, and if a son, then an heir through God.

— **Galatians 4:6-7**

Every time I read this verse; I am reminded of two things I experience with my own kids as a father.

The first is the utter heartbreak I feel when I sense one of my children striving for my approval. I'm not talking about the joy a child gets when their dad is "proud of them." I mean those moments when my children wonder if they are accepted by me because they have let me down in one of their actions. It hurts me, because I SO LOVE them. And I want them to live knowing that love is granted to them because they are my children, not because of their performance or actions.

This is why Paul says, "you are no longer a slave, but a son." Slaves have to earn their keep; sons live in the inheritance of their Father. When we come into the family of God by faith, we are to live as children of God and not under the slavery of "earning" His love.

The second is the joy of being called "Dad." One time one of my children called me "Jeremy." I told them not to and they said, "but that is your name." I looked back and said, "Yes, but here is what you need to know. Lots of people call me 'Jeremy,' others call me 'pastor,' others call me 'friend,' but there are only five people who can call me 'Dad.'" It is a joy and delight to have that special designation from my five children.

This is the privilege that our faith in Jesus gives us. Our relationship with God, while it includes all of these things, isn't only defined as God the creator, the judge, the all-powerful, etc. It is defined in the intimacy of a loving father. We are His children, loved in His family, and free to enjoy Him unconditionally. The power of simple grace is the power of unconditional love and acceptance because of faith in Jesus.

Bible Reading Question:

Is there anything from the reading that speaks to you today? If so, what is it?

Points for Pondering and Prayer:

Did you have a difficult relationship with your dad? Does it make it hard to understand this passage? If so, invite the Holy Spirit into your heart to heal those hurts.

Ask the Holy Spirit to show you what true unconditional love is like.

Perhaps, ask the Holy Spirit if you need to forgive your earthly dad so that you can experience the love of your Heavenly Father even more.

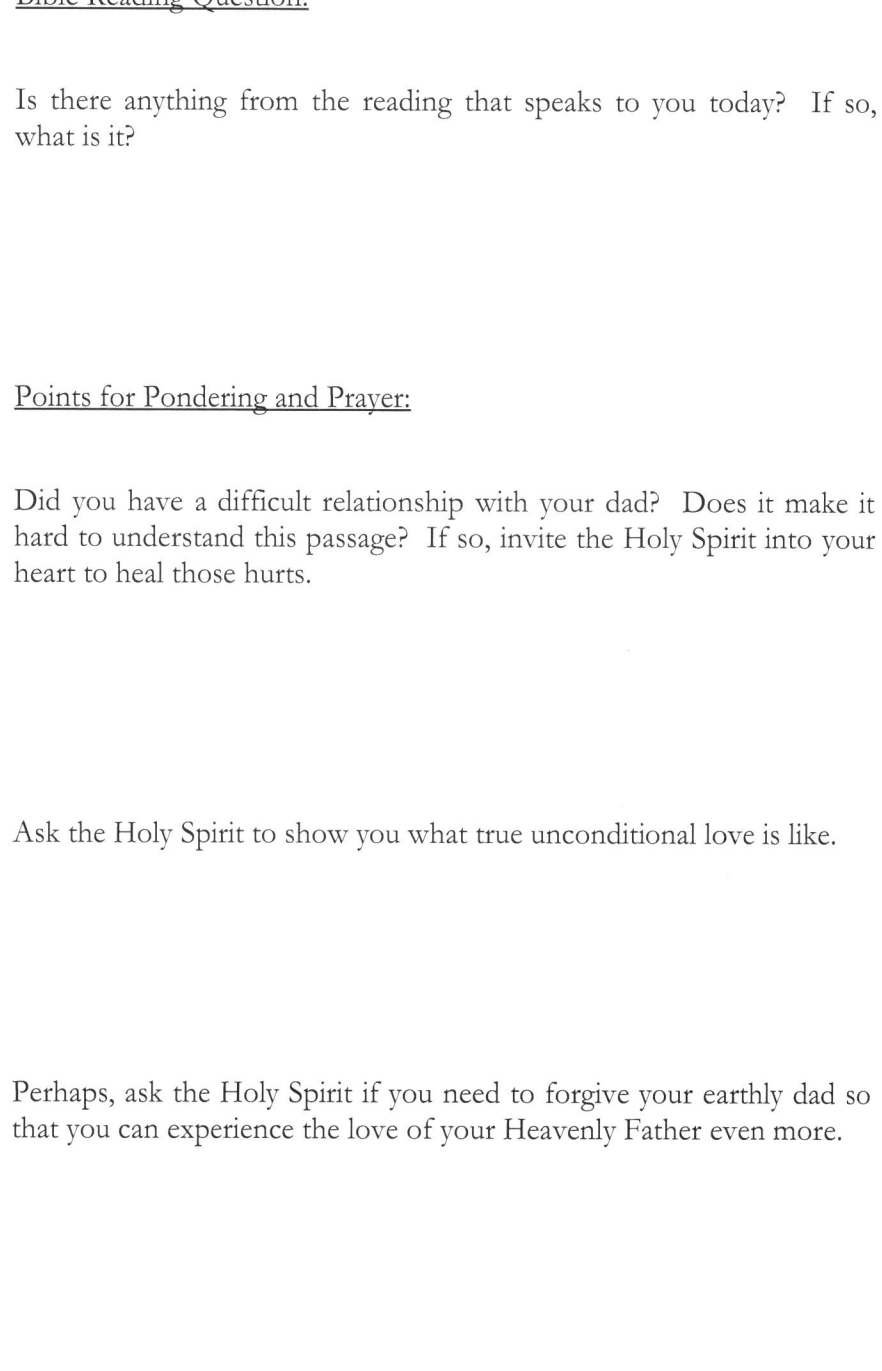

Week 4

Galatians 4:8-5:1

Grace Above All Curses

Because of Faith, Jesus Alone Determines My Destiny

But now that you have come to know God, or rather be known by God, how can you turn back again to the weak and worthless elementary principles of the world, whose slaves you want to be once more?

— Galatians 4:9

Week 4, Day 1

Bible Reading: Galatians 4:8-11

But now that you have come to know God, or rather be known by God, how can you turn back again to the weak and worthless elementary principles of the world, whose slaves you want to be once more?

— Galatians 4:9

The "it's up to me" lie takes on many forms. For most of Galatians, Paul is addressing the "follow the religious rules" lie that the Jews applied to the Old Testament Law. "You can obey the Law, that can save you, it's up to you."

However, most of the Galatian church did not have a Jewish background, and here Paul is addressing the same lie, but in pagan form. In the pagan world, there were two ways that the "it's up to me" lie took root. The first was in spiritualism and the second was in appeasement.

The view of appeasement assumed God (or the gods) were angry with them. Therefore, they took it upon themselves to appease that anger. This could be through sensuality, through sacrifice, through chants and prayers. But, when the gods were angry, people had to take action. It was up to them to appease the gods.

Spirituality took on the notion of connecting with the spiritual world. Meditating, prayer, understanding the spirits, etc. If you could figure out how to commune with the spirits you could appease the spirits. Again, it's up to you. And Gentiles were leaving the burden of the Law to run to their former spiritual, appeasement lives at their peril.

I can imagine that Paul's heart leapt for joy when he heard James, the brother of Jesus, say at the Jerusalem Council, "We should not make it difficult for the Gentiles who are turning to God" (Acts 15:19).

Paul knew that any additions to the simple grace of God would send the Gentiles running to the familiarity of appeasement instead of the confusion and complexity of the Jewish Law. But the simple grace of Jesus is powerful enough to change our lives and habits. It draws us into a relationship with a loving God, not the constant fear of an angry God.

Bible Reading Question:

Is there anything from the reading that speaks to you today? If so, what is it?

Points for Pondering and Prayer:

When things are going bad in life, do you automatically assume you have done something wrong to invite God's judgment? Is this race or "it's up to me" appeasement?

How would our perspective change if every day — good, bad, ugly — were looked at as an opportunity or a gift of grace?

Week 4, Day 2

Bible Reading: Galatians 4:12-20

What then has become of your blessedness? For I testify to you that, if possible, you would have gouged out your eyes and given them to me.

— Galatians 4:15

I love the rawness of Paul's emotion in this paragraph. So many times when we are "perplexed" by the circumstances of life we try to wash it clean with faith-sounding fakeness. Paul is raw, emotional, and blunt.

But… what is going on with "gouging out your eyes?"

Many Bible scholars believe that Paul either had very poor eyesight or was functionally blind during most of his ministry and it may have started with his stay in Galatia.

There are several reasons for this conclusion. First, prior to coming to Galatia, Paul had been stoned to the point of people thinking he was dead (Acts 14:19). He then talks about his "bodily ailment" which had something to do with his eyes in Galatians 4. Many years later, Luke records that Paul did not recognize a high priest when he was on trial in Jerusalem (Acts 23:4-5). Given Paul's background as a Pharisee, it would seem strange for him to make this mistake without an eye problem. Finally, on several occasions Paul talks about writing the ending of his letter "with my own hand" (Col. 4:18, 2 Thesis. 3:17, 1 Cor. 16:21), and in Galatians he says his greeting has "large letters" (Gal. 6:11). Both of these are consistent with an eyesight problem that would have made ancient writing very difficult.

It must have been frustrating for Paul to write of the revelation of the gospel with a "seeing" problem. After all, when Paul first met Jesus, he was struck blind (Act 8:8), then he was later healed and recovered his sight (Acts 8:18). Now, at his moment of seeing the gospel advanced among the Gentiles, he is again functionally blind! If it had been me, I would have had some serious thoughts about being under a curse of some sort.

Yet, Paul didn't. Instead, this suffering probably confirmed his message. After all, Jesus had said of Paul, "I will show him how much he must suffer for the sake of my name" (Acts 8:16). Paul understood that if his Savior suffered to bring him into relationship with God, it was Paul's honor to endure suffering to bring others to know Jesus. Suffering is part of simple grace!

What freedom!

You see, if suffering or lack of suffering is up to us and our actions, then it brings bondage. It would mean that every time something bad happens to us, we would assume it was our own fault. Our bad behavior brings suffering, our good behavior brings favor.

Yet, Paul was advancing the gospel and suffering. It is grace. It is freedom. It was part of God's plan. It was not a judgment of Paul's actions. All he had to do was embrace the suffering and continue to do the will of God. And so he found sufficient, simple grace in his darkest days.

Bible Reading Question:

Is there anything from the reading that speaks to you today? If so, what is it?

Points for Pondering and Prayer:

How would you grade your life right now? 1 is really bad, 10 is great?

Do you associate the goodness or badness of life with God's blessing or judgment? What does that say about your level of surrender?

Embrace the grace — spend some time thanking God for where you are in this moment in life. Ask God to show you His grace. If needed, ask God how to find sufficient grace in a time of suffering (need more inspiration, check out Paul's words in Philippians 4:11-13).

Week 4, Day 3

Christ redeemed us from the curse of the law by becoming a curse for us... how can you turn back again to the weak and worthless elementary principles of the world, whose slaves you want to be once more?

— **Galatians 3:13a, 4:9b**

The subtlety of the "it's up to me" lie is really amazing. For example, the enemy was able to take such a beautiful plan of God to save the world by faith, and the beautiful Law of God to help guide us in His ways, and turn it into a self-righteous, prideful fundamentalism that invites us to trust ourselves as our own gods! Wow!

Likewise, the enemy can take a super powerful reality like faith, blessings, and freedom from curses and turn it into an "it's up to me" trap. How many times have I thought: "if I'm having a bad life, I must have cursed myself; if I am having a blessed life, I must be blessed?" But this simply isn't the heart of Jesus' grace. Actually, at times it can be a form of mystical appeasement. "If I say the right things, God will be pleased with me and cause the right things to happen to me."

Simple grace understands that Jesus became a curse for us and died under a curse to defend us from all curses. Likewise, His death and resurrection secured every blessing of heaven for us for eternity. When we put our life in His hands by faith, we can rest confidently that nothing in our life happens outside of His guidance, plan or redemptive control. A life of simple grace exalts the plan of God, it does not frustrate it.

Look at Paul as an example. He saw hundreds of miraculous healings (even his own), and yet, he lived mostly blind throughout his ministry and under constant physical affliction. He saw members of the government's elite military force exchange their oaths declaring Caesar as god for faith in Jesus, yet some of his closest friends betrayed him. When he came to know Jesus he was probably a very wealthy man who had amazing social and political status, he would die a poor prisoner accused of being a traitor. God rescued him from death countless times, yet he ended up being executed. Was his life the sum of all the "blessings" or "curses" spoke over him? No. As he says at the end of his life...

For I am already being poured out as a drink offering, and the time of my departure has come. I have fought the good fight, I have finished the race, I have kept the faith. Henceforth there is laid up for me a crown of righteousness, which the Lord, the righteous judge, will award to me on that Day...

— **2 Timothy 4:6-8a**

Paul exalts the plan of God. Why? He understood that a life of simple grace submits itself to Jesus. What comes next is simply part of "the race" and an opportunity to give God more glory. A gracious glory that comes from keeping the faith.

Points for Pondering and Prayer:

Do you "fight the good fight" of your life from a place of knowing your place of eternal blessing in God, or from a place of fear that you might mess up?

Do you rejoice in your trials or fight against them? Read James 1:2 and ponder this question more.

Ask the Holy Spirit to reveal simple grace to you again.

Week 4, Day 4

<u>Bible Reading:</u> Galatians 4:21-31

Paul is continuing to argue that those who are of faith are part of the Promise to Abraham in Genesis 12. And if we are part of the Promise, we are the true sons of Abraham. To do so, he uses an example, or allegory, from the Old Testament story of Abraham's two sons (you can read about it in detail in Genesis 16-17, 21).

Paul's point is quite simple. The descendants of Ishmael, the son of Abraham that was not part of the Promise of God, are just as much sons of Abraham according to biology as the sons from Isaac (son of Promise) who became the Jews. Biology is not the point. The point is the Promise. God's Promise was one of faith that would make us right with Him (Gen. 15:6). That promise would be fulfilled in the lineage of Isaac and then the Jewish nation (Genesis 17:17-18), that would finally come about in Jesus (Gen. 17:7). It is a promise of faith.

So, allegorically speaking, just as one son was not the legitimate heir of the Promise of Abraham, and should be cast off, so also the "it's up to me" slavery of the Law is not the legitimate heir of the grace of God and should be cast off in favor of the freedom of Jesus.

> *So, brothers, we are not children of the slave but of the free woman.*
> **— Galatians 4:31**

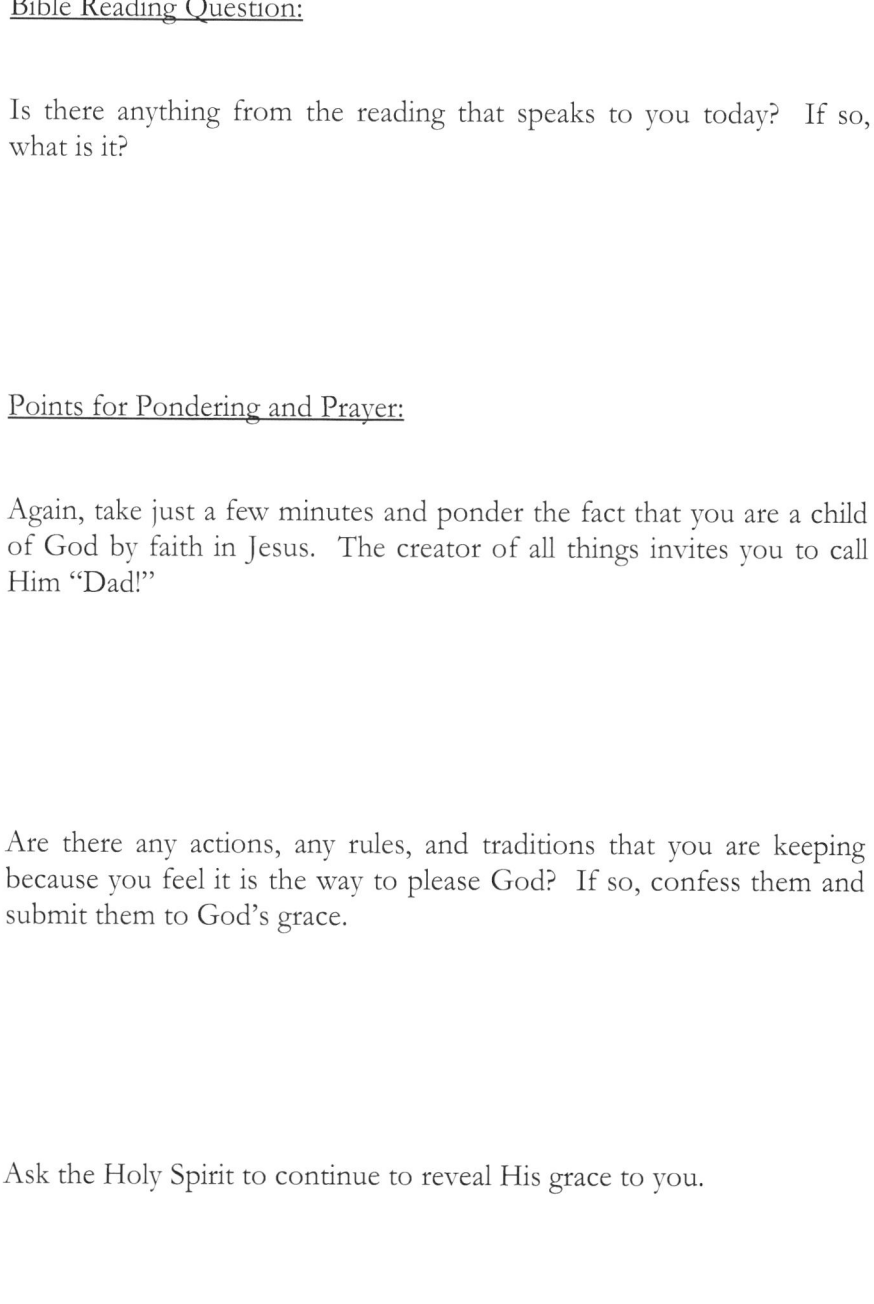

Bible Reading Question:

Is there anything from the reading that speaks to you today? If so, what is it?

Points for Pondering and Prayer:

Again, take just a few minutes and ponder the fact that you are a child of God by faith in Jesus. The creator of all things invites you to call Him "Dad!"

Are there any actions, any rules, and traditions that you are keeping because you feel it is the way to please God? If so, confess them and submit them to God's grace.

Ask the Holy Spirit to continue to reveal His grace to you.

Week 4, Day 5

For freedom Christ has set us free; stand firm therefore, and do not submit again to a yoke of slavery.

— **Galatians 5:1**

Here again we find one of the more amazing verses in the Bible. Why did Jesus set us free? So that we could be free!

Think about it this way. Let's pretend you are a conservationist who has found an endangered wild cat that has had its leg broken by a hunter's trap. It was once free, but due to the curse of the hunter it is now in danger of losing its life.

So you capture it and imprison it in your animal compound with the goal of nursing it back to health. After a few weeks you release it into the wild. Why? For freedom. So the wild cat can fully be a wild cat again.

Now here is the thing. Any true conservationist would be heartbroken if that endangered wild cat tried to return to captivity after it had healed enough to be free. It would have meant that the conservationist did not do her job. She had imprisoned an otherwise free animal.

The verse above is Paul, the gospel-of-grace conservationist, saying, "be free, don't come back to captivity." The simple grace of God is SO freeing.

It frees us from the bondage of our sin! We are forgiven and can live without shame.

It frees us from the "it's up to me" captivity of trying to impress God by doing all the right things when we are wounded failures.

It frees us from trying to be hyper-spiritual or trying to appease Him when He is angry.

It allows us to be who God wants us to be — men and women being remade in the perfect image of Him. Free to love, free to enjoy, free to live.

How? By faith. Faith is simply what you do with what you know. Faith is living out our trust and obedience to God. You see, after simple faith, obedience is not about impressing God, but it is about enjoying God. We obey because we know God can be trusted. We obey because we know God's ways work. We obey because we are free. And we obey in the power of the Holy Spirit, not in self-effort to measure up to some "rule."

That is freedom. And starting now in Galatians 5-6, Paul will show us exactly what living in the freedom of grace looks like practically in our lives.

Points for Pondering and Prayer:

How does the idea of a God who wants you to feel free to enjoy Him and life really feel to you?

If it is uncomfortable, ask the Holy Spirit to reveal what the true, enjoying-God freedom of grace is really like.

Week 5

Galatians 5:2-25

The Lifestyle of Grace

Depending on the Holy Spirit to Live by Faith and Work Through Love

For through the Spirit, by faith, we ourselves eagerly wait for the hope of righteousness. For in Christ Jesus neither circumcision nor uncircumcision counts for anything, but only faith working through love.
— Galatians 5:5-6

Week 5, Day 1

Bible Reading: Galatians 5:2-6

For through the Spirit, by faith, we ourselves eagerly wait for the hope of righteousness. For in Christ Jesus neither circumcision nor uncircumcision counts for anything, but only faith working through love.

— Galatians 5:5-6

Paul is shifting from his theological argument for simple grace into the lifestyle of grace. But he wants to make one final plea to the Galatians to forsake the Jesus-plus-the-Law message of the Judaizers.

Here he encapsulates his argument well. Our acceptance before God (righteousness) comes by faith through the Holy Spirit. Thus, obedience to the Law (circumcision) is not the issue. Rather, the requirement of Jesus is "faith working through love."

Paul is going to get to the real meaning of "faith working through love" in the next few verses, but it is essentially his paraphrase of Jesus' great commandment, "Love the Lord your God with all your heart… and love your neighbor as yourself" (Mt. 22:36-40).

Faith is the ultimate expression of loving God with everything. Faith says, "God is who He says He is, I will trust Him with everything." Faith is the ultimate act of surrender — it is relying on the truth of a God we can't see to guide us through a cursed world that we can see. There is nothing more loving than to say to God, "I believe You are who You say You are." Faith is the power on which simple grace functions.

But here is the catch. Faith is "working through love." How do you love a God you can't see? As we will see soon, Paul will say it is by loving those you CAN see. The demonstration of faith is to love our brother the way God loves us, to be in unity with our brother the way God unites Himself with us, to be good, kind, forgiving, patient, self-controlled with our brother because God showed all those things towards us.

Do we love out of obligation or under a requirement of the Law? No. We do it out of gratitude for our Savior and in the power of the Holy Spirit. That is how faith is lived out, through loving others.

Bible Reading Question:

Is there anything from the reading that speaks to you today? If so, what is it?

Points for Pondering and Prayer:

If someone examined your life, could they see your faith by how you love those around you? Do the people who know you best respect you the most?

How well do you love difficult people?

What is one thing the Holy Spirit is asking you to do to show love to someone today?

Week 5, Day 2

<u>Bible Reading:</u> Galatians 5:7-12

But if I, brothers, still preach circumcision, why am I still being persecuted? In that case the offense of the cross has been removed. I wish those who unsettle you would emasculate themselves!

— **Galatians 5:11-12**

This is some of Paul's strongest language in any of his writings. How dangerous does he see the "it's up to me" lie to be? Better to be operated on in a painful area than to submit to it! But I want you to notice some incredible logic that Paul uses here.

Paul says that the evidence of his gospel being true IS the persecution that he, and other Christians, are experiencing. The message of the gospel, a message of "you can't do it yourself; you are hopeless, you need Jesus" is so offensive sooner or later it will invite persecution. Therefore, if Paul is persecuted, but his opponents aren't, Paul's gospel is more true. Why is this? Why does Paul say this?

Because at the center of the Judaizers message is one that says obedience is equal to physical or worldly blessing. If you obey the Law, God will reward you with worldly blessing — peace, riches, wealth, prosperity, etc. In other words, your quality of life is up to you. If you are persecuted, there is a flaw in your life.

At first, this sounds good. After all, God's ways work and when we follow His principles, we often see success. But Paul knows that at the heart of their philosophy, the Judaizers are really preaching a way to manipulate God. Our slavery to the Law is there to manipulate God into rewarding us. When rewards don't come, it is up to us to change something in order to appease Him and get more rewards. What bondage! No wonder Paul is so strong with his language! This kind of thinking is a trap.

But grace came by a perfect God-man who suffered and died. God's well-pleasing Son was required to suffer to extend us grace. A grace that requires the relinquishment of all power, control, or self-effort. A grace that requires us to be helpless and desperate before the Almighty. It is going to offend. And that offense will cause the same type of persecution that His well-pleasing Son experienced. Persecution and trial often means we, as "little-Christs" (or Christians), are living the gospel.

Bible Reading Question:

Is there anything from the reading that speaks to you today? If so, what is it?

Points for Pondering and Prayer:

Let's examine our hearts one more time. Do you equate the "good" in life with "good" actions on your behalf? Do you equate the "bad" in life as "punishment?" Then who is in charge, your actions or God?

Ask the Holy Spirit to again reveal His grace to you.

Week 5, Day 3

For you were called to freedom, brothers. Only do not use your freedom as an opportunity for the flesh, but through love serve one another. For the whole law is fulfilled in one word: "You shall love your neighbor as yourself." But if you bite and devour one another, watch out that you are not consumed by one another.

— Galatians 5:13-15

So, we are five weeks and three days into this study, and I am sure a few of you have thought, "But Jeremy, if you don't have the Law or the rules, how do you know how to behave? Are we really free to live as we please?" Great question. Paul is going to answer it.

The short answer is, "no." We aren't free to live as "I" please. Simple grace changes our hearts in order to live in a way that pleases Jesus. After all, what is more freeing than living the way that the One who freed us lives? Paul summed it up a few verses ago when he said, "faith working through love." Faith is the love language to God. Love is the proof of its work in our life. This is what Paul is saying.

"Do not use your freedom as an opportunity for the flesh." Grace doesn't mean do what you want. That makes you God. The essence of grace and faith is to make God more God in your life. Not to make you more God of you. So how do we know when we are acting in faith or acting according to the flesh? One simple question: Are we loving our neighbor?

Grace demonstrates our great faith in Jesus by exercising His great love for others. We love a God we cannot see through our actions towards people we can see.

After all, this is the essence of what Jesus did for us. Jesus loved a Heavenly Father who (while on earth) He chose not to physically see by loving sinful people whom He could see. He lived with them, healed them, cared for them, elevated the disenfranchised, welcomed children, spoke kindly of them, fed them, and ultimately submitted to a brutal death and false accusations on behalf of them. And what was

His great statement at the height of His execution? "Father forgive them."

Loving our neighbors and stewarding our freedom well simply means loving those around us in the same way Jesus loved us. And this begins with those in the household of faith.

Points for Pondering and Prayer:

Take a few moments to think about some of the ways Jesus has loved you. Especially ponder those places where you know you didn't deserve His love.

Considering these things, how is the Holy Spirit directing you to love others?

Week 5, Day 4

Bible Reading: Galatians 5:16-24

But I say, walk by the Spirit, and you will not gratify the desires of the flesh... But the fruit of the Spirit is ...

— Galatians 5:16, 22

I've grown up being taught the fruits of the Spirit all my life. Yes, I know... I'm supposed to be more loving, more joyful, more self-controlled, etc. Oddly enough, it sounds like a list of laws I am supposed to do to be like Jesus.

Wait? What? Didn't we just spend four chapters talking about how laws kill? Has Paul essentially done the same thing, but just put the word "Spirit" in front of these laws?

At first glance it might seem like it. But there is one real difference. The Holy Spirit.

The fruit of the Spirit is not a "to-do list" of things we are supposed to accomplish. And it's certainly not a list of things that are "up to you" to do. Rather, they are a list of things the Holy Spirit does in you as you submit to Him.

When you encounter life, you will have a choice. Do it on your own (the flesh) or submit to the leadership of the Holy Spirit (walk by the Spirit). When you submit to the Spirit by faith, He works His fruit in you. When you need love, seek the Spirit in faith, the Spirit provides love by grace. The same for joy, peace, patience, etc. You rely on Him and He works in you.

Again, we see the example of simple grace. All that is required is your faith. The power to save you is by grace. The power to free you from the Law is by grace. Even the power to live for Jesus through the Spirit is by faith. Why? Because in this way, God gets ALL the glory.

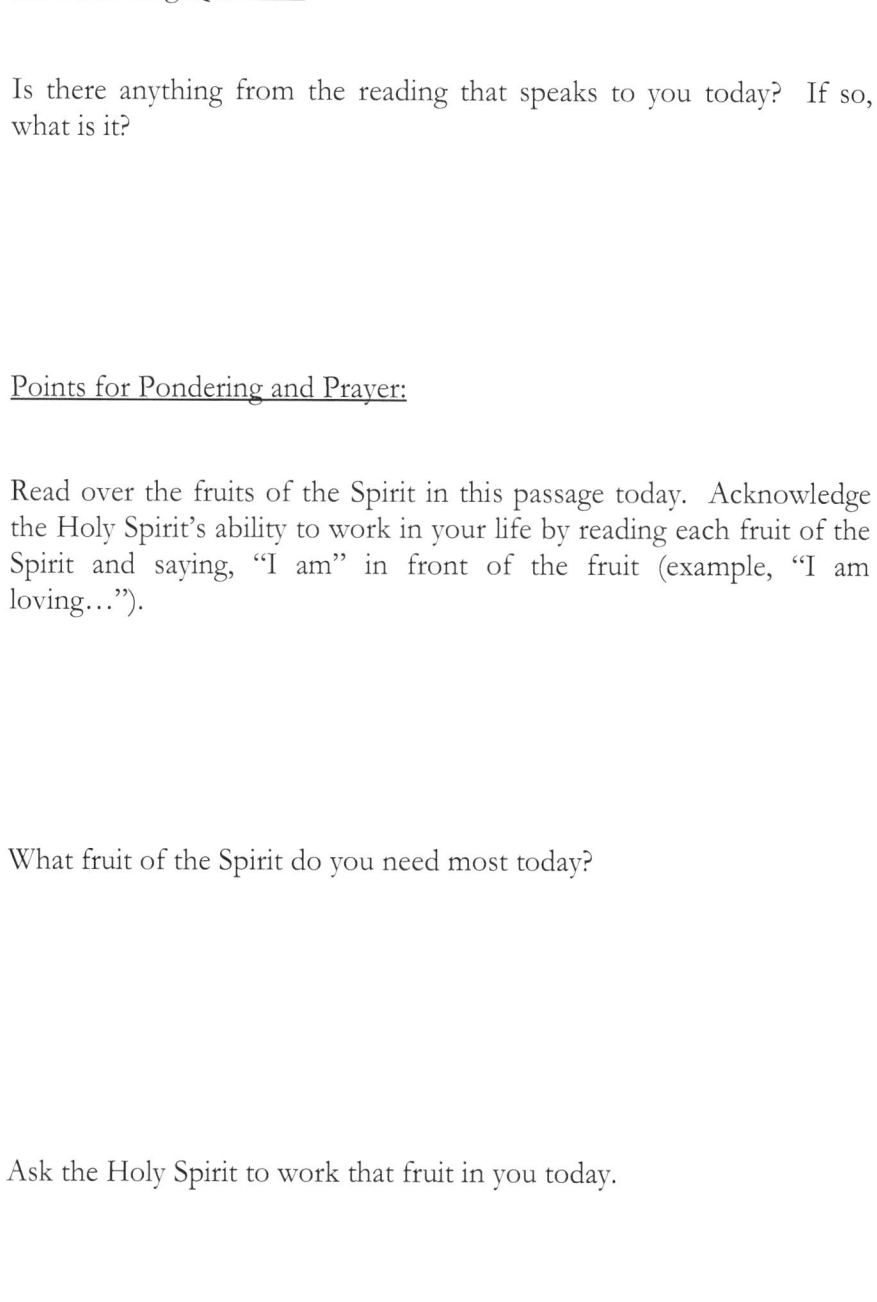

Bible Reading Question:

Is there anything from the reading that speaks to you today? If so, what is it?

Points for Pondering and Prayer:

Read over the fruits of the Spirit in this passage today. Acknowledge the Holy Spirit's ability to work in your life by reading each fruit of the Spirit and saying, "I am" in front of the fruit (example, "I am loving…").

What fruit of the Spirit do you need most today?

Ask the Holy Spirit to work that fruit in you today.

Week 5, Day 5

Bible Reading: Galatians 5:25-26

If we live by the Spirit, let us also keep in step with the Spirit. Let us not become conceited, provoking one another, envying one another.

— Galatians 5:25-26

What causes pride, provocation, or envy? Thinking we are better than someone, smarter than someone, or that someone is better off than I am. In other words, these emotions are all generated by comparing ourselves with others and thinking "it's up to me" to be like or better than that person.

Paul's solution? Just please the Spirit.

"If we live by the Spirit, let us also keep in step with the Spirit." In other words, the Holy Spirit knows exactly where you need to be in life. So focus on staying in step with Him because if you are where He is you are exactly where you need to be. When you keep pace with the Holy Spirit in your life, you will not worry about where others are in life.

Again, notice the power of simple grace. No comparison games. No "look at that person and what they are doing." What about you?

Simple grace is just you, faith, and the Holy Spirit. Grace is the power of acceptance. And as you walk with the Holy Spirit's guidance in your life, you live in the power of full acceptance no matter the circumstances. If you are where the Spirit wants you, you are in the right place.

Bible Reading Question:

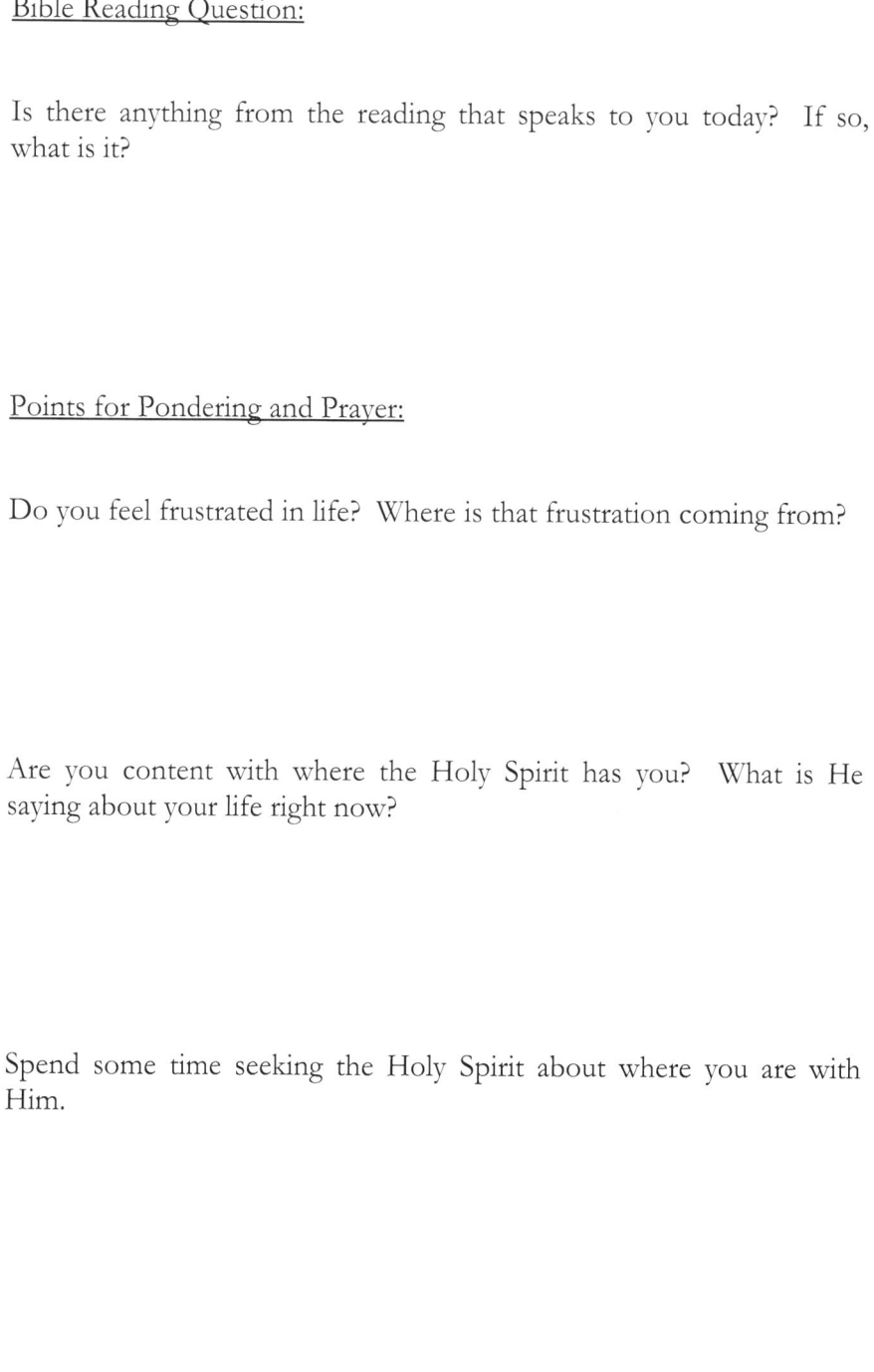

Is there anything from the reading that speaks to you today? If so, what is it?

Points for Pondering and Prayer:

Do you feel frustrated in life? Where is that frustration coming from?

Are you content with where the Holy Spirit has you? What is He saying about your life right now?

Spend some time seeking the Holy Spirit about where you are with Him.

Week 6

Galatians 6:1-18

The Law of Grace

Simple Grace Asks, "What Does Love Require of Me?" in Every Aspect of My Life

Bear one another's burdens, and so fulfill the law of Christ.
— Galatians 6:2

Week 6, Day 1

Brothers, if anyone is caught in any transgression, you who are spiritual should restore him in a spirit of gentleness. Keep watch on yourself, lest you too be tempted. Bear one another's burdens, and so fulfill the law of Christ. For if anyone thinks he is something, when he is nothing, he deceives himself. But let each one test his own work, and then his reason to boast will be in himself alone and not in his neighbor. For each will have to bear his own load.

— Galatians 6:1-5

Paul continues to apply simple grace to loving our neighbor. This is what the "law of Christ" refers to, "loving our neighbor as ourselves." Look carefully how he applies it.

#1 — We love our neighbor when we restore him or warn her about his or her sin. However, love conducts itself with gentleness. Why? Because we are all sinners. Notice the grace. Love rebukes and does not ignore sin. But love does so from a place of weakness and empathy.

#2 — We love our neighbor when we bear their burdens. This is actually a financial encouragement. We love when we see a brother of ours in need and contribute to those needs. But again, notice the simple grace. We don't help them in pride at our own success, we help them knowing that everything we possess is from God and should be used to accomplish God's purposes.

#3 — We love our neighbor when we provide for our own needs. Again, this is a financial discussion. Paul is saying that our goal should always be to have a work ethic or the financial wisdom where we can provide a living for our own family. That way we are not living dependent upon the charity of others. We should "each bear our own load" and be prepared to "bear one another's burdens." Again, simple grace. God works His character of wisdom, excellence, diligence into our hearts, we apply it to our work, and we provide for our families.

In these simple areas, confronting sin and in financial provision, simple grace asks the questions of the Holy Spirit, "what does love require of me?" Then it follows the Spirit in its answer. Restore the sinner. Help the struggling. Work hard to provide for my family. That is faith working in love.

Points for Pondering and Prayer:

Are you struggling with a sin pattern that needs to be defeated? What does love require?

Is there someone you know who is struggling with sin and needs to be restored? What does love require?

Is there a burden God is asking you to contribute towards? What does love require?

Are you doing all you can to live free and responsibly with your own finances? What does love require?

Week 6, Day 2

Let the one who is taught the word share all good things with the one who teaches. Do not be deceived: God is not mocked, for whatever one sows, that will he also reap. For the one who sows to his own flesh will from the flesh reap corruption, but the one who sows to the Spirit will from the Spirit reap eternal life. And let us not grow weary of doing good, for in due season we will reap, if we do not give up. So then, as we have opportunity, let us do good to everyone, and especially to those who are of the household of faith.

— Galatians 6:6-10

Paul continues in his practical application of loving our neighbor in response to the work of simple grace in our lives. Let's look at what he says.

#1 — We love our neighbor when we provide for our spiritual leaders. "The one who is taught" is the congregation. "The one who teaches" is the church leadership. Paul here (and other places) essentially says that a congregation may reach a size that it is good to have a set of full-time leaders to care for them. When that happens, we love our neighbors by providing for their spiritual care. This is a benefit to the members of the congregation.

Paul then adds just a little bit of a warning, "God is not mocked," and encourages us to sow to the "things of the Spirit." Paul is encouraging the Galatians to remember two things. First, that advancing the Kingdom of God is the church's first priority. So, sowing into advancing the gospel is of vital importance — including financial importance. Second, Paul is also reminding us that God sees the investment into the Kingdom and will not be "mocked" by letting those investments go unrewarded; "the one who sows to the Spirit will from the Spirit reap eternal life."

#2 — We love our neighbor when we do good at every opportunity. When we know we can, and we know the Spirit is telling us to, we do the loving thing. We don't back down, make excuses, or ignore the problem. We do good when we show love at every opportunity, we have to love others.

#3 — We love our neighbors when we prioritize the household of faith. Paul clearly cares about the poor. He had told us that he is "eager to do" so (Gal. 2:10). But he also knows that as a family, we love and care for our family. So being passionate about loving the people of our local church is an example of faith working itself out in love. It is simple grace.

Points for Pondering and Prayer:

What would love have you do when it comes to providing for the spiritual leadership at your local church?

Is there an opportunity for you to do good to someone you know today? What would love have you do?

Is there a member of your congregation that you know could use some cheering up or help? What would love have you do?

Week 6, Day 3

Bible Reading: Galatians 6:11-16

But far be it from me to boast except in the cross of our Lord Jesus Christ, by which the world has been crucified to me, and I to the world.

— Galatians 6:16

Paul, in his own hand, writes the single greatest description of simple grace in this letter. When it comes down to it, grace is about who gets the glory and who gets the credit.

Living the "it's up to me" lie by trying to do all the right things brings me all the credit. After all, if I succeed, if I live a perfect life and obtain a right-standing before God because of my perfection alone, I simply prove that I don't need Jesus. I get the credit, Jesus gets none.

If I'm living the "it's up to me" lie by trying to appease God in order to find peace, prosperity, and blessing, then again, I get the credit. After all, if I succeed, then I have conformed God to my wishes and desires by my actions. In short, God had to respond to me.

If I'm living the "it's up to me" lie by finding success and happiness apart from God, then again I get the credit. I am my own god, and show that life can be lived without Him. I get the credit.

But simple grace is the opposite of all of these things. In fact, it kills (or crucifies) these things so that Jesus gets the credit. Simple grace is the ultimate self-actualization because it realizes that true peace, happiness, and right-standing before God can not be found in this world or obtained by me with all my flaws and failures. After all, if I let myself down (and all of us know that we let ourselves down), why would we think we don't let God down?

So we surrender. We believe God. We tell Jesus to take over and be our provision. We give up and give it all to Him. The result? He gets ALL THE GLORY for what happens to me, for me, in me, and as a result of my life. Simple grace and simple glory. So, who gets the credit for your life?

Bible Reading Question:

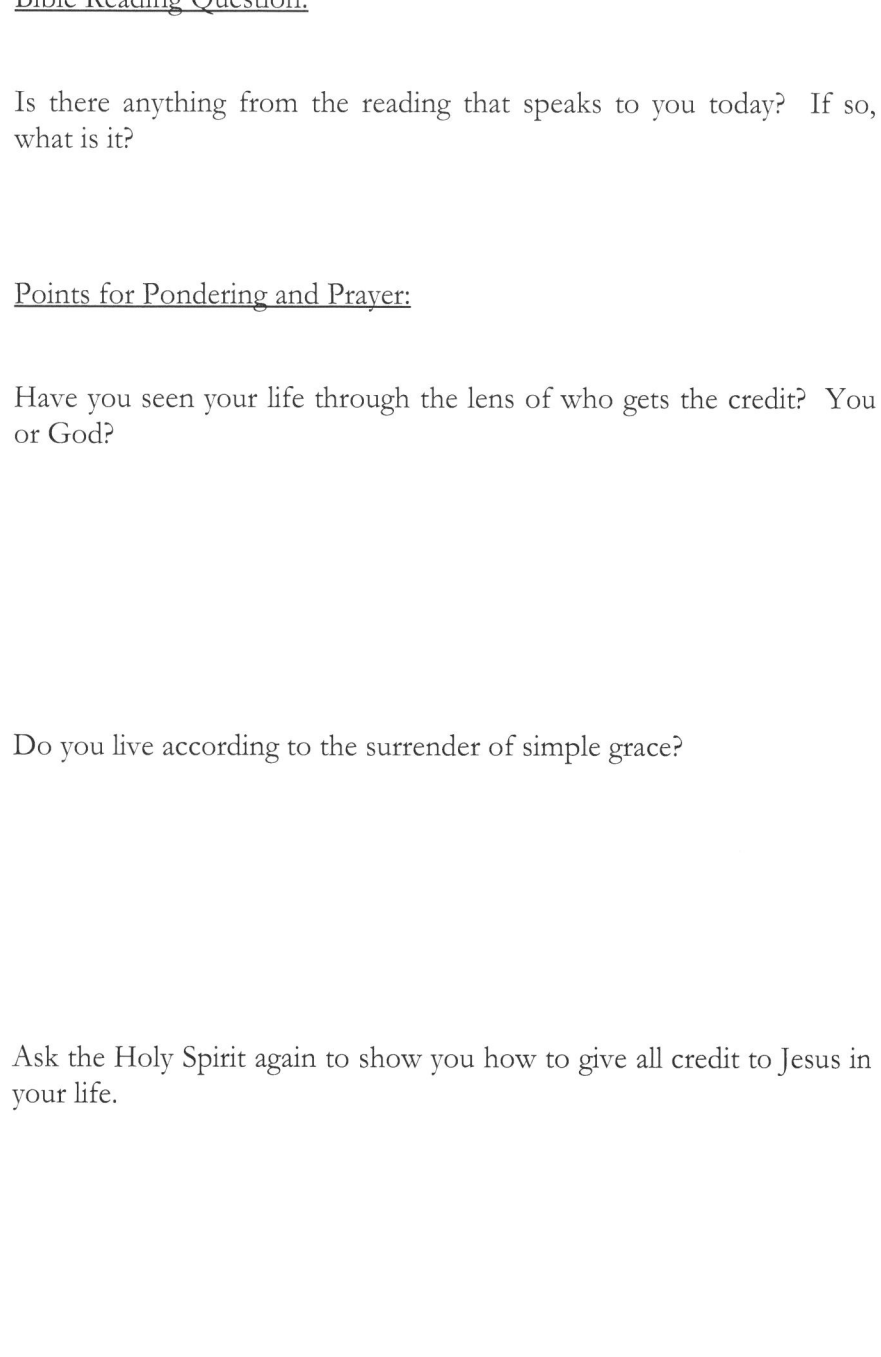

Is there anything from the reading that speaks to you today? If so, what is it?

Points for Pondering and Prayer:

Have you seen your life through the lens of who gets the credit? You or God?

Do you live according to the surrender of simple grace?

Ask the Holy Spirit again to show you how to give all credit to Jesus in your life.

Week 6, Day 4

From now on let no one cause me trouble, for I bear on my body the marks of Jesus. The grace of our Lord Jesus Christ be with your spirit, brothers. Amen.

— Galatians 6:17-18

With this, Paul closes his letter. Notice two simple things about these powerful words.

#1 — Paul tells us his purpose. He is going to live for Jesus no matter what. The suffering he has already endured are "the marks of Jesus." Not surprisingly, at this point in Paul's life, those marks had just begun. He would be imprisoned many more times, tortured many more times, betrayed many more times, put on trial many more times, get sick many more times, and, ultimately, would bear the mark of execution for Jesus. But he turned each one of these circumstances into a mark of glory. Each trial was a blessing. Each ailment, a sign of love. Each bit of suffering, a joy. Why? Because it gave more credit to Jesus. He was an instrument of glory.

#2 — Paul pronounces a final blessing. His heart's desire was for the Galatians to know Jesus Christ in their spirits. That His Holy Spirit would unite with their spirit and not be shaken by a do-it-yourself gospel. Rather, that they would find freedom in the love and relationship with their Heavenly Father.

So what about you? Are you willing to be "marked" for Jesus? Are you enjoying the relationship-only, faith-only, grace-only life in Jesus?

Points for Pondering and Prayer:

What is one thing you learned from today's reading?

What is one thing you have learned from the Galatians study?

Ask the Holy Spirit to continue to work simple grace in your life.

Week 6, Day 5

The grace of our Lord Jesus Christ be with your spirit, brothers. Amen.

— Galatians 6:18

Looking Back

Often, we don't realize how far we've come unless we take a pause to look back at the journey we've been on. I know I have had many seasons where I am constantly looking at my "to-do" list and often forget to look back at the "done." When I do… "wow" is all I can say… I am amazed at all God has done for me.

It's that same way looking at the study of Galatians. We need to take a look back and see what God has done in our lives through the study of His Word. In many ways Paul's theme in Galatians is *Simple Grace: Get It, Give It, Live It.* Let's look at the journey.

Simple Grace: Get It – Galatians 1-2

Paul reminds the Galatians that his encounter of grace came with his personal interaction with Jesus Christ – not simply living through the lives or wisdom of others. Notice in these passages that Paul was bold and confident in the gospel he was preaching because he had personal experience with the Lord. It wasn't something he read in a self-help book, a how-to book, or some great advice he got from a friend. Paul made room for God and God met with him. When we connect with God by faith, we have the grace of His wisdom and input for our daily struggles.

Simple Grace: Give It – Galatians 3-4

Paul argues that Jesus is the offspring of righteousness promised to Abraham, and the fulfillment of Abraham's blessing is the fact that Jesus' salvation is offered to the Gentiles (all people). The message of Jesus was never just for "us," whoever our version of "us" is. Our lives are impacted by grace so that we can give it away!

Simple Grace: Live It – Galatians 5-6

If grace isn't working practically in our lives, do we really have it… and is there a way to see if we need to cling to God more? As a friend of mine once said of this passage, "The fruit of the Spirit is like a check-up at the doctor:

1.) Are you loving others like Christ?

2.) Are you experiencing joy in your life?

3.) Is your heart in a place of peace?

4.) Do you exercise patience with others?

'The cross deals a constant blow to our pride and self-reliance.' … In our failure, God creates a need for Him. Take a spiritual check-up today. Replace self-reliance with the fruit of God's strength and Spirit working in you." Grace is part of our practical, day-to-day life!

I hope you have enjoyed the study of Galatians. May the simple grace of Jesus forever transform your life and may you never be the same because of your encounter with it. If you have a story you would like to tell me about how Jesus' grace has changed you, please email me at: info@hccgoshen.org.

Simple Grace Message Series

If you would like to listen to Pastor Jeremy's messages in his Simple Grace series through Galatians, please visit:
https://www.hccgoshen.org/simple-grace

Final Notes

Special thanks to Nancy Diener who assisted with the editing, formatting, and publishing of this book.

For more information on Harvest Community Church, please visit our website: **www.hccgoshen.org**.

Made in the USA
Lexington, KY
22 July 2019